MW01283675

FASTEN YOUR SEAT BELTS

CONFESSIONS OF A FLY GUY

By

David Edmondson

For class 8 Northwest Airlines Feb. 15, 1992

We were given the wings to fly

Acknowledgements

For Clare Myers, Christine Kiel, and Michael Randall, without your friendships, this book could not have been written.

For Eric Dansie, who lived through most of this with me. Your support and friendship have been everything.

For Cindy Held Szlasa from the Gulf Air training, You and Karen have known me longer than anyone. Your friendship with Karen was a true inspiration to us all.

For Patti LaCross, my first flight with you made me realize what caring is all about.

For Marilyn Pitts to fly with you was a joy, and please know I am grateful to know you.

Contents

Prologue

It was October 2022. I was comfortably seated in Comfort+ on my flight from Atlanta to Rome. I was on my way to take an inaugural sailing from Rome to New York City. Just after takeoff and the hot towels had been delivered, I could see the beverage carts being positioned in the galley. I sat back and waited to see if there were any familiar faces working on the cart. It had been some time since I had worked one of those carts, making my way down the aisle, going somewhere—anywhere my schedule dictated.

There is something about having been a Flight Attendant that never leaves you. It is not just a job, not just the repetition of duties, or the constant need to be alert and aware of anything that might happen at any given moment. It was a way of life unlike any other, setting one apart from the real world. It was not nine-to-five or a set routine. It was something that I am sure every Flight Attendant who did the job long enough made concessions in their lives to make it all work.

There were moments when I felt I could not deal with one more delay, cancellation, crying baby, or angry passenger, but I always believed the next flight would be better. I would go to a favorite city, meet up with a special friend in Europe, Asia, or India. I would fly with a friend, plan a new layover, meet a special passenger, or help someone through a personal crisis. Every flight was different, and if they were challenging, I was comforted in knowing I would never have the same group of passengers again. The next flight might be just as challenging, but it would be a different challenge with a different group of passengers. There were times when my feet hurt, the uniform felt constricting; however, I always felt as if I was doing something special. That I was making a difference in the smallest of ways to total strangers that I would never see again.

When I first started my flying career, I did not realize you take yourself with you wherever you go. You could absorb the training and accept how you needed to react to any given situation, but it was your own instinct that dictated the outcome. Certainly, I began flying when the golden age of air travel was long gone. Every decade, the airline business seemed to dumb down or change. Deregulation, mergers, bankruptcies, hijackings, aircraft changes, layoffs, new hiring, 9/11, terrorist attacks, and airport screenings all created changes and challenges to the industry. But one thing that could not change was the need for Flight Attendants. Safety still depended on the human element—for pilots to fly the planes, and for Flight Attendants to ensure your safety.

There are thousands who have served as Flight Attendants over the years, both active and retired. Some flew longer than others, some left bitter or jaded, while others made this a lifelong career. One thing for certain: we each had the common denominator of turning the dream of flying into reality, each with a unique story to tell. This one is mine!

Chapter 1

I Can Dream, Can't I?

Growing up in a small rodeo town thirty miles south of Ft. Worth, Texas, I could not seriously contemplate what it would be like to be a Flight Attendant. I could only dream and wait. I remember clearly when the brand-new DFW airport opened between the cities in January 1974. It was an exciting time for the Metroplex, and shortly after, American Airlines moved its operations and headquarters to the new airport. Airlines began hiring males in the cabin only after 1972 when EEOC laws changed for minorities, women's rights, and gender inclusivity. I remember the Ft. Worth Star-Telegram article detailing American's hiring of males in the cabin in the early seventies.

I graduated from high school in 1969 and made plans for career choices, but the knowledge of knowing I could at some point have a career as a Flight Attendant stayed with me. In the immediate term, however, I chose a technical field—Dental Technology, which worked very well for me at the time. I received offers from laboratories all over the country as it was a very new field and short of trained technicians. In 1975, I accepted a job offer with a dental laboratory in Beverly Hills, California. The laboratory was very well known and did exclusive work for The Dentist to the Stars, where we constructed crowns and bridges for many Hollywood celebrities, writers, and politicians in Southern California. Our laboratory worked on Academy Award-winning actors, singers, and songwriters, novelists, famous hairdressers, and politicians. I was a dental ceramist and was often in charge of matching porcelain caps to the natural shade of existing tooth structure. It was rewarding and challenging, but like everything, it became second nature. After eleven years at the lab, I needed more in my life than working on study models of the famous or near-famous. I went to work part-time in sales at the Neiman Marcus store in Beverly Hills in Men's Furnishings. I served many of the same clientele I had in Dentistry, but in a much different capacity. It served its purpose, but during this time my father passed away, and I had a strong pull back to my home and to Texas. I had gone through several fractured relationships, which seemed harder and harder to hold onto in the changing late seventies and early eighties.

I bought a house and moved to the eastern side of Ft. Worth, settled in with a new relationship, and continued to work at a dental lab locally. Still, something was missing. My true destiny was to fly. Not simply because of the so-called glamour, but I needed to be in constant motion. Unfamiliar places, fresh faces, new horizons. I made up my mind I was going to do this; I just did not know quite how to go about it.

This was a challenging time in aviation. Some airlines were dying slow deaths, some were hanging on, just barely, while others were trying to consolidate and hope for better days. Braniff International Airways, a Dallas-based company, had an image of glamour and haute couture with their Emilio Pucci Flight Attendant uniforms. Their rainwear uniform consisted of a plastic space bubble which, to say the least, received the desired results as they walked through an airport. With hindsight, I often wondered how they could have secured those things in the cabin—certainly not in an overhead bin. Unfortunately, with the airline's image of glamour and innovation, a true aviation pioneer came overspending and corporate greed, which led to the demise of a wonderful legacy in air travel. Braniff International shut down operations on May 12, 1982. There were to be many more legacy airlines to follow.

I did not let the economics of the industry dampen my motivation. At this point in my mind, becoming a Flight Attendant was the career for me. I was more determined than ever to make it happen. My first choice, or the best fit for me, would be American, as it was my hometown airline, closest to me, and would be the best in location, followed closely by Delta, which was always considered a top-notch carrier based in the South. My third choice was Continental Airlines, based in Houston. I felt it would also be a good fit for me. It would all come down to the process. Little did I know the process would be the biggest obstacle, almost insurmountable from the get-go.

Even during these tough economic times, I decided to apply with as many airlines as I could in hopes the right fit would come along. I received a reply from TWA first and felt this was a good omen. I fit the qualifications and returned the completed application to Kansas City and patiently waited to receive a reply. In the interim, I received my first reply from Delta, which listed the qualifications required to be accepted into their training program, along with an application. Yes, I had 20/20 vision, I could swim, I could lift thirty pounds, and my weight was in proportion to my height. As I continued to read the application over and over, I was stunned. It was clear. My height was not in proportion to my weight. I was six feet two inches tall. It was hard for me to comprehend that I was vertically challenged and too tall to perform the duties of a Flight Attendant with certain companies. Delta would only accept male Flight Attendants who were a maximum of six feet tall. Many of the largest carriers in the U.S. were flying the L-1011 aircraft, which had a galley downstairs below the passenger cabin, which was an extremely limited space, and if too tall, you could not stand fully upright. This I understood, but it certainly would be a problem going forward.

I was crushed to realize the obstacle of my height might kill my chances. A couple of weeks later, I received the same devastating news from American. I crossed my fingers and waited for something positive from TWA, as they did not seem to have the same height restrictions. It was a couple of weeks later that I received the letter with the TWA letterhead on a white envelope. More unwelcome news. The letter thanked me for my interest in TWA, but due to current conditions in the airline industry, TWA had stopped all hiring at this time. I was encouraged to reapply in another twelve months. For the moment, I was nowhere. I was determined to fly, but how or when would come down to luck and timing.

It was during this time I got to know a beautiful girl at the gym where I worked out in Dallas. She had been a Pan Am stewardess and later a Flight Attendant recruiter for the company when the airline was still flying high. She was always encouraging, always smiling, supportive, and a great disco partner on some late nights out. "Do not wait around," she would say. "Look into charter carriers while you wait for the mainlines to start hiring again. At least get in the air, and it is much easier to get hired if they know you have done the job before. Keep in mind, the hardest part about the job is getting hired!"

This was a time when the Flight Attendant position, male or female, was the most applied-for job in America. There would often be three hundred thousand applicants for four hundred positions.

I began to research charter companies and smaller legacy airlines with more limited flight schedules. I began sending out applications and was consumed with paperwork. Oddly enough, most of the charter carriers or the Airlink smaller airlines did not seem to care how tall you were, only if you were able-bodied and could open the door in an emergency.

I bought a new conservative charcoal suit, a conservative tie, and listened intently to my friend from Pan Am about the interview questions—what might be asked and how to respond. My first interview was with Skybus Airways in Columbus, Ohio. The entire process was chaotic and rushed. We started out in a group of twelve, were asked a few collective questions, and then some were thanked for coming, and half the group was sent in one at a time for a one-on-one. Something about the fellow who I sat across from struck me as preoccupied and unprepared. I was nervous myself, and his delay in asking me basic questions was even more disturbing. I answered his questions better than they were asked, but overall, on the flight home, it did not feel right.

I responded to a couple of interviews for Airlink Airlines, which flew primarily prop planes to Midland and Tulsa. The interviews went well, but it was just not the kind of flying I was interested in.

During the Skybus interview, I met a couple of girls in the lobby before we went in for the interview. We were able to network a bit, and they filled me in on the hiring scene as they perceived it on the East Coast. I related my limited experience in the entire process and hopefully filled them in on what was going on with airlines throughout Texas. I ended up taking the bus back to the airport with the girl from Pittsburgh. She had similar feelings about the interview we had just endured. She felt, as did I, it was a waste of time. She did, however, tip me off to an airline that was growing, and she knew they were holding interview sessions in Philadelphia. The name of the airline was Gulf Air—not the Saudi Arabian Gulf Air, but the American Gulf Air, which was headquartered on a small island off the coast of Louisiana. "I never heard of that one—has anyone else?" I asked. I thanked her for the tip and said I would see her there if the timing was right. We were all just gasping for air.

Chapter 2

Be Careful What You Wish For

It was a cloudy and overcast day when I arrived at Philadelphia Airport after my American Airlines flight. I used the travel voucher provided by Gulf Air Inflight, taking the earliest departure out of DFW in time for my 1 PM interview. During the flight, I went over and over in my mind how this interview might play out—questions and jumbled thoughts of what to say and when to say it. The more I thought, the more nervous I became. This was uncharted territory for me. The thoughts and questions tumbled over one another. They must need Flight Attendants, or why would they send me a flight voucher in the first place? I did not have experience. Did they want females and were just filling their legal obligation to interview or consider males? Where did this airline fly? So many questions in my head, and with each thought and question, my nerves set in. I was early, so I stopped for a coffee, which did little to control my jitters. I asked at the airport ticket counter, which displayed a blue and gold banner reading GULF AIR. I was directed to a door and told to go downstairs. I reached a check-in desk, lined with office cubicles, and was instructed to be seated. The Inflight Manager will be with you shortly, I was told.

A young woman emerged from an office cubicle and extended her hand. She was smiling and warm, and she made me feel a bit more at ease. I was struck by how much makeup she had on. She had blue eyeshadow all the way to the brow and very red lipstick. Her hair looked as though it had been recently permed. She was very well put together but certainly not in the conservative way I was expecting. "You're David Edmondson, right?" she asked as she looked down at her papers and offered me a chair across from where she was seated. "I'm in charge of Flight Attendant recruiting and training. I understand you're interested in a Flight Attendant position with us."

The interview was off to an exceptionally good start, and the recruiter struck me as friendly and not intimidating. She asked me several questions about experience, why I wanted to do this job, was I willing to relocate, and would I be prepared for six weeks of training here at Philly Airport with hands-on training of the aircraft at JFK. I was personable and willing. She asked me if I had any questions, and certainly, I had many. Where did the airline fly, what types of aircraft, and how many Flight Attendants were already flying? She said I met the requirements of the airline, and she closed the interview. "You'll hear from us either way within a week, David, and thank you for meeting with me today." She shook my hand, and the interview was over.

I took several deep breaths as I made my way back up to the terminal to take my return flight home. It was difficult to comprehend what decisions would be made from this interview. It went well, it was straightforward, concise, but she left me with a lingering doubt about the outcome. I guess I'll know within a week.

Two days later, back in Ft. Worth, I received the call. I was hired by Gulf Air, and I would need to report to training in three weeks. A complete hiring packet would be sent by mail, and I was to follow the instructions carefully. It would require physical and background checks and, of course, completion of the training. It was not what I had originally planned, and there were so many unknowns, but I was going to be a Flight Attendant.

Back in Dallas, as I sat with my beautiful former Pan Am recruiter and friend, I filled her in on the process so far. I would have so many adjustments to make, not the least being going from a six-figure income down to almost minimum wage. Also, with Charter, I would have flight benefits with my company only and reduced rates on other carriers, so commuting would not work. I would need to domicile at my base. In my conversation, I found myself sugar-coating what I needed to do rather than what I wanted to do. It was all new and exciting, and with my optimism, I was sure I could make it work. She reminded me it was a beginning, that this job or any Flight Attendant position should be counted as a win. "The whole industry is in a downturn," she reminded me. We both agreed that with this company, foreign destinations are real possibilities as the airline has worldwide authority to charter flights wherever needed. There were military charters to trouble spots, or rescue workers or firefighters to fly for disaster relief, and best of all, the group charters to all the sun destinations—the Caribbean Islands, Europe, or Scandinavia. It was a small airline with a small imprint and less than twenty aging aircraft, but it would be my first steps in the air.

I asked my friend, "You are still young and beautiful—do you think you will fly again someday?" "You know, David, when I flew for Pan Am, which seems like so long ago, it was another world up there. Class, couture uniforms, standards, the newest planes, fine wine, and cuisine, impeccably dressed passengers. I have often thought about it, but I don't think it's for me anymore. But that is me, and now this is your time to make your mark in the air. Believe me, years go by as those carts roll down the aisles, so don't miss a minute of the experience. Just remember, as they always told us at Pan Am, it's always the journey, not the destination."

Chapter 3

Theory of Flight

The Holiday Inn at Philly Airport was to be the hub of our training for Gulf Air. We were assigned roommates, two to a room. It was an adequate but run-down facility under the overpass bridge heading downtown. My roommate, who was from the Bronx in New York City, fancied himself as a ladies' man, and if behavior was any indication, he was. He and I had absolutely nothing in common other than our training. I tried to avoid him as much as possible, but straightaway, it was to be a long six weeks. Our instructor was a stout English lady who was no-nonsense, curt, and could be described as basically charm-free. She was efficient, by the book, and required your full attention.

Early morning classes consisted of airport codes (the three-digit code for each airport we serviced and those that we might need to use), which we had been required to learn even before leaving home, types of aircraft, and at the time, Gulf Air flew primarily 727-100/200. It was most important to learn what keeps an aircraft in the air, known as the Theory of Flight, which consists of specific elements working with or against one another. Lift, weight, drag, and thrust working in tandem is what keeps an aircraft in the air. We were required to learn all aspects of emergency equipment: fire extinguishers (Halon, H2O)—the difference and its use, First Aid Kits—what they contained and how to use what they contained, AED—its use and location, life vests, life rafts, and on and on. We were tested continually on each element and had to maintain at least an eighty-two score for passing each exam. These were eight-to-five days with a lunch break factored in. The food was the expected burgers and fry-ups, but as demanding as the days were, there was an element of moving toward that common goal of being on those aircraft. There were only six males out of thirty in the class, so it was clear we were there out of necessity rather than preferential choice. Many in the class had flown with other airlines, mostly charter, which had folded or went through downsizing, so many just wanted to keep flying until something better came along. This being my first airline, I did not really know what to expect or how I should act or react to the situation, the class training, and the social aspect of being in such close quarters for such long and exhausting days. I'm sure I asked all the wrong questions, and too many as well, but this was a learning experience in multiple ways. I was more comfortable in the training class than being in the room with a roommate playing loud music, slamming doors, and having girls in and out at all hours. It was said he was having a fling with one of the supervisors, but who was I to care? I just wanted to pass the training, stay focused on what I had to do, and fly away as soon as possible.

In week three, we began the medical part of the training with CPR practices, first aid, medical situations, and we practiced and were evaluated in CPR on dummies on the floor. As serious and important as all this was, there seemed to be something so comical about this procedure, at least for me. I looked across the room and could see the guys bent over, breathing into these lifeless plastic dummies. The girls with their skirts hiked up, and all of us sweating and straining to bring simulated life into an inanimate object—but we all learned, and learned it well. Many of us were to fall back on this procedure in actual situations, and this is something that has always been a trigger when needed.

Into the fourth week of training, it felt as though a collective fatigue had set in. This was about the time I noticed some of my clothes began to disappear. I thought initially it was my imagination, looked everywhere, and decided to forget about it. It was the intensity of the training and my state of mind. What was there to do about it? I had my suspicions, but I kept them to myself.

We needed to remain focused, but the long days, the overcast sky, the cold mornings, and the difficult personalities began to wear thin. Coming from the highly technical field of dental technology and an environment of total support and communication, it was hard for me to adjust to chaos. I was the fourth oldest in the training class; there was another element of disconnect from the mostly twenty-something mentality. I'm sure I took things more seriously than others, but I never did things in half measures, and it was important to me to learn all that I could. Our training class began with just under thirty applicants, and by the fourth week of training, we had lost five—some continually failed the exams, others voluntarily left for personal reasons, and some may have failed the drug test or the physical.

In the fifth week of training, we were bused to a motel in Queens near New York's LaGuardia airport for actual training in an unused training facility of a major airline adjacent to the airport. Same room assignments, same personal challenges, but things were getting very real, more visual, more tangible, nearer to being on an actual aircraft. We were required to go down the slide, mock water ditching in a pool, life vests, life rafts, overwater equipment, and emergency evacuation commands. We found ourselves waking in our sleep to these commands. Timing was everything. In an actual emergency, you would only have so many seconds to get every passenger out of an aircraft. This was the time that the clarity of responsibility came into focus, and there is that time for every Flight Attendant when they become aware of what they are really on that aircraft for. This was that time for me.

It was back to Philly and the Holiday Inn for the final week of training. This would consist of uniform fittings, and what was called grooming. Later, there was instruction on service and serving etiquette. I was prepared to take it all in and get on with it.

The grooming class was a bit of fun. The guys were told we could not wear makeup—no surprise there—but we were also told we could not have beards or hair below our collars. The top shirt button would always be buttoned, and the tie properly tied. This reinforced my disdain of neckties for men. I always felt two of the most ridiculous fashion innovations were neckties for men and pantyhose for women, which I came to acknowledge both were to be must-wears in any Flight Attendant uniform. The girls were instructed to wear heavier makeup, as the cabin lighting often gave off an artificial glow. This explained why my original recruiter was so heavily made up during my initial interview. That day, the naturally beautiful girls had on too much makeup and looked odd to me and the other guys, while the girls that already wore too much makeup applied even more. After we all started flying the aircraft, most of the girls went back to their usual routines, and I never grew a beard.

Several of the online Flight Attendants came to class to model the Gulf Air Uniform. It was simple and well-designed. It did not seem to have any of the usual trappings of older uniforms with braids or epaulettes. For the guys, it was a simple three-piece suit with coat, slacks, and vest, white shirts in a light dove grey. The tie was a grey and maroon stripe. The girls had skirts and vests with white blouses and correlating bow ties. We had black all-weather coats and black service aprons. We were all measured that day, which was a good indicator that most of us would be around to wear the uniform.

The night before our last training day, several of my classmates all went down to the lounge and disco in the hotel. We had made it through some difficult training, and we would receive our uniforms and be scheduled to work training flights on real aircraft to actual destinations. There were five of us who had bonded during the process. I was a little older than most, but there was a beautiful girl from Puerto Rico, a real spitfire who was always the life of the party; another guy from upstate Pennsylvania; a girl from Delaware; and two girls from Boston. Gulf Air had three Flight Attendant bases: Boston, Detroit, and Philadelphia. Our training class had some young, bright, and intelligent men and women. There were two girls in their early twenties who were as close as sisters, both had worked for other charter airlines which had folded, but these girls already had much international experience. I enjoyed conversations with these two on some of the bus rides, and I looked forward to flying with them on future trips. It would be years later that we would reconnect and appreciate who we were then and where life was to take us. This was the case for several of my Gulf Air classmates.

We would not receive our base assignments until after our training flights and graduation. It would be fine with me to be assigned to the Philly Base as I was at least familiar, having trained there. We assumed the Boston girls would be based back in Boston, but it all came down to the company's needs.

I tossed and turned that night—so much to remember, so many adjustments to make, so many doubts about tomorrow. Had I made the right choices, done the right thing, learned what I needed to know? About this time, a crack of light came through the door as my roommate staggered to his bed. At least I would be done with this roommate situation.

Chapter 4

Wings

I was nervous on the day of my assigned check ride. Our class had not yet received our uniforms, and for each of us, the check rides were the decisive step to becoming all that we had trained for. I was told to wear dark slacks, a white shirt, and a dark tie. Our uniforms would be distributed, and our graduation ceremony would take place after all check rides had been completed. Some of my classmates had heard gossip about the instructor who was evaluating our initial check rides stacking pillows or blankets over some of the emergency equipment to throw us off during our preflight check. I tried to mentally prepare for whatever might be thrown at me. I knew the equipment, its location, and my responses. My thinking was that, in the most dreaded situations, anxiety is often worse than reality. This turned out to be the case, as I handled the preflight check, and the instructor introduced me to the working Flight Attendants. Later, the captain and his crew hurriedly came on board, gave me a sideways glance, introduced themselves, and took their seats in the cockpit. We boarded a full flight of passengers. The inflight instructor had me place the girt bar into the floor fittings to arm both forward doors.

The inflight instructor would remain on the flight to monitor my behavior and assess my performance. This was a Philly-Nassau Bahamas turn. We would take a full flight of passengers to Nassau, have a four-hour ground sit, and bring a full load of passengers back to Philly. I was told by the lead Flight Attendant to assist with passenger boarding, assist in the beverage and drink service, handle the cabin pickup, and help in any area required. I was willing to do all of that, but I was not clear that I would not be doing it all at once. The concept of working as a crew was new to me. I had much to learn.

It was a given that most charter flights would be a full aircraft. The fare prices were low, and every seat would be taken unless some unseen emergency or no-show left a vacant seat. That did not happen often. We were flying the 727 aircraft, which had never been equipped with beverage or meal carts, so Flight Attendants had to run beverages off trays and hand-deliver 149 or 189 meals, depending on the aircraft configuration. Depending on experience and agility, the most meal boxes a Flight Attendant could handle at one time would be five. I started with three and upped my game to four as I became more comfortable. Halfway through the flight, I felt as though I saw my own tail go by, as the service seemed so frantic and chaotic. I perspired and ran up and down that aisle. I finally got a smile from the Flight Attendant working the aft galley, who gave me my first word of encouragement. "We were all new once, hon," she drawled. "You're working way too hard. It will get easier, I promise," she said. She was from Arkansas and had a very heavy accent, but looking back, this is one kindness I have chosen to remember.

We landed in Nassau and deplaned the passengers down the airstairs onto the tarmac. As the cabin door opened, I could see the tropical sunshine and feel the warm, balmy air of the island. I had been to most of the Caribbean Islands on a whirlwind vacation in the late seventies, but I was now a working crew member earning my wings. Most of the crew decided to go into the terminal for duty-free shopping or just to get off the aircraft, but I felt it best to stay on board and focus on the return trip. On the return, it would be easier going, for I would at least not have to second-guess what was to come next. On the ground, I rested in the back of the plane and observed the supervisor filling out paperwork seated up front, which I felt was the evaluation of my first flight. I felt confident I had done the best that I could do.

Graduation day was a day we could collectively feel gratified for the six weeks and all we had been through. It was time to apply all we had learned, hoped for, and worked for. We were all in uniform, and the director of inflight pinned our wings individually. Some of my classmates who lived locally had family members there to congratulate them. I did not have anyone to celebrate with or to be congratulated by. I was proud of myself for pursuing a dream that was important to me. Most of my friends and family back home thought I would regret giving up a lucrative career for such a low-paying job. Only my mother supported and encouraged me to follow my dream. She was the one I called that day.

Philadelphia was to be my base assignment. During my first weeks of flying, I took a commuter room in one of the motels near the airport until I could scope out something more permanent. One of the commuting

Flight Attendants I did not know very well approached me about an apartment in a residential area close to the airport. Several Flight Attendants had apartments there, and she asked if I would be interested in sharing. She was a very reserved and quiet person, so I felt it would be a good fit. We took the plunge, and I had some of my things moved up from storage in Texas. She would commute to her home on days off, so we never really had a lot of time together in the apartment. Several of my classmates also rented apartments in the buildings because of the desirable location. There were three of the female Flight Attendants sharing one unit directly across from my apartment. One morning, as I was preparing to work a Caribbean trip, I looked out the window and happened to see my former training roommate taking out a bag of trash from the very unit across the greenspace of the three Flight Attendants. He happened to be wearing my favorite nightshirt, which had mysteriously disappeared during training.

To work any given flight requires several steps before arriving at the aircraft. We had to make a call two hours before our flight to confirm our intent to work the flight. We were then required to sign in at the inflight services desk to reconfirm we were present before heading to the aircraft. We had to present our security badges and were let onto the aircraft by ground staff servicing our company. Once on the aircraft, we bid positions by seniority, which was our hire date. As I was usually the most junior on any given trip, I was required to work in a position the other crew members did not care to work. Senior Flight Attendants often chose to take the lead position, as they liked to serve the needs of the cockpit as well as the forward cabin of passengers. The lead Flight Attendant oversaw the aircraft after the cockpit crew and was responsible for the service flow, serving the cockpit crew, medical emergencies, unusual occurrences, and unruly passengers. The lead was also responsible for all forms and documentation of unusual incidents, catering discrepancies, and any aircraft irregularities. On rare occasions, the lead Flight Attendant role was passed down to me. I was aware that on Gulf Air, the cockpit guys did not like to be served by the male Flight Attendants, which was never spoken but always acknowledged. The lead Flight Attendant also had the discretion to delegate certain tasks to other Flight Attendants, so when I served as lead, I would have one of the girls serve the cockpit. In hindsight, this sounds very sexist, but some things were slow to change. Often, when I was lead Flight Attendant, I had my share of medical emergencies, so I learned quickly to fall back on my training. Most emergencies did not require diversions, but some did. This was another time I was grateful for Flight Attendant teamwork. Training was really the key in any crisis.

One of my early trips was a Cozumel turn off the eastern coast of the Mexican Yucatan Peninsula. We would fly down with a leisure group, sit for five hours, and make the return to Philly. The aircraft was at full capacity, and during the meal service, we were short two passenger meals. Naturally, the passengers were upset. We did all we could to try and salvage the situation. We served the passengers two of the designated crew meals, which was not particularly satisfying to the passengers or the crew. We did avert the crisis, but we were short of crew meals in the process. The pilot did arrange for crew vouchers in the airport, so after deplaning, the entire crew went into the airport restaurant.

We were all exhausted from the early morning departure, a full cabin, short meals, and we were hungry as well. The mariachi music was festive in the restaurant, the chips and salsa were delivered, and we felt it would be a fun meal. It would all be covered by food vouchers. We all ordered some Mexican concoctions off the menu, which was in Spanish, and waited for the food to arrive. Hot plates were set in front of us. I picked up my fork to take my first bite when I heard the co-pilot scream and shove his plate across the table. "What the fuck," he shouted. We all looked in his direction. "Take a look at that plate," he said. In with the cheese and meat, things were moving. He called the waiter, but what could be done? To be served a plate of maggots is enough to put one off food, then and in one's memory. We purchased what packaged snacks we could take back on the plane, and the crew meals we were boarded for the return to Philly went mostly untouched.

I struggled to adjust to the flying routine. My biggest adjustment was being on the East Coast—the weather, the food, and the people. I developed friendships with several of the junior Flight Attendants, as we could commiserate with one another about our trips, the company, and our colleagues. Our group of five would sometimes get together on our days off and take the train into Washington or New York. I drove my car up from Texas, a ragtop Jeep, which gave us transportation around Philly or for close day trips. One of the girls that lived just over the Delaware line suggested that we go to Rehoboth Beach in Delaware.

It was a beautiful summer day, so we piled into the Jeep and headed for the beach. It was two guys and three girls. The top was down, we blasted the radio, and we felt the breeze on our faces. We reached the beach around noon, walked the boardwalk, and had lunch outdoors. The sea was sparkling, the weather was warm, and it was a great afternoon. Most of us had trips the following day, so we started back early. As we left the beach, we noticed huge black clouds forming on the horizon, and I commented that we might need to hustle to get back to Philly before a storm blew in. Too late. We were heading right into the storm. Half an hour into the drive, huge rain mixed with hail began to drench us. I pulled over to put the top up, but I had left the removable doors back in Philly. With the rain came an icy wind, which blew through the Jeep. We were all in bikini tops and tank tops and soaked to the skin. I recall looking back in the rearview mirror at our Puerto Rican spitfire. Her hair was soaked and stringing across her face, and her mascara was running down both cheeks. The Jeep rocked back and forth in the high winds. I feared I would need to pull over, but everyone insisted we keep going. We all needed to be back at base. It was early evening when we at last pulled into the apartments. We were frozen, soaked, but safely back.

Chapter 5

Nothing Lasts Forever

My trips got better. There had been another training class in the seven months I flew, but only one. This seemed a bit odd, but I did not question reality at this point. I was working in the Bahamas, Nassau, Bonaire, Curaçao, Trinidad and Tobago, the Netherlands Antilles, Cancún, Cozumel, and all points in the Caribbean. I worked military charters sometimes, from Nashville to Pensacola or Richmond to Ontario. The girls liked to bid for the sports team charters—NFL teams, NBA, any, or all who needed to be flown to their games. I worked one Sports Charter and hoped I would not have to do another. Huge meal trays had to be served, an open bar, bedlam, and they almost always wanted to be served by the ladies.

Some trips would be turns, but most would be layovers, which I came to enjoy. I flew the lead position often, usually by choice or sometimes by seniority pass down. I still got attitude from the cockpit, and I still delegated their service to one of the girls, but it no longer annoyed me. At this point in time, I had learned to practice acceptance, sometimes by choice, other times by necessity.

I have always had a fear of water where I could not see the bottom. There was something about not knowing what might be down there that was disturbing to me. Looking back, this may have stemmed from when I was just five years old at Eagle Mountain Lake, and I fell off a log into the water. Had my mother not been there, I surely would have drowned. For whatever reason, this has always been a fear. I am not a beach person; I do not really like sand in my shoes, glare in my eyes, or heat on my skin. However, here I was working for an airline that flew primarily to island and beach destinations. People from the north loved these trips. The aircraft were always full—it is the myth of something so different from their day-to-day. The rain, or the snow—who could fault them for wanting a sea breeze under a palm tree?

I was working lead with a crew of some of my besties to Cancún. The Puerto Rican spitfire and a couple of the Philly girls I really loved to be around. It was always fun, always a party, and we worked together so well. It was to be a twenty-eight-hour layover at a magnificent hotel on the beach. It had been such foul weather when we left Philly; we were all looking forward to the sun and sea. The girls made me promise I would come down to the beach, as they knew that ordinarily, I would sit by the pool and never go to the beach. I did as I promised. We all oiled up and spread out on our towels. Shortly after lying in the hot sun, they all decided to go into the water. They stood at the edge of the surf calling my name to the point that I felt embarrassed not to join them. I made my way to the edge of the surf. I could just get my feet wet. The water was so clear, so blue, the balmy breeze, and I could see the bottom. They all swam further out, calling to me to join them. I felt a bit silly and thought, "Why not?" I stepped into the surf up to my neck and was ready to take a plunge when out of the corner of my eye, I saw something float past. My eyes widened when I realized this was raw sewage. Disgusted, I bid a hasty retreat, cursing under my breath. The girls followed me out of the water. We all decided to move to the pool for the rest of the afternoon. Practicing acceptance was indeed becoming second nature to me.

The island layovers were a welcome break from the weather back in Philly, but things had become a bit routine for me. I was often homesick, sometimes lonely for the familiar part of my life I had left behind. I noticed subtle changes in the company as well. The airline industry was still in its negative downturn, with no relief in sight. I am certain this is why some charter companies seemed to stay around. I became aware that some of our bases were beginning to lay off Flight Attendants, especially the Detroit base. Possibly it was a restructuring of the flying, and the company wanted to shift more flying to the Boston and Philly bases. That made no sense, however. Why not just relocate Flight Attendants rather than lay them off? This was a time when crews flew together, and the questions began. No one knew what was really going on, so there was increased gossip and speculation.

I began to see more trips on my schedule with one of my classmates. She was just senior to me by age, a tall, willowy blonde. She was always cool and well put together, and she had a history of flying with multiple airlines in the past. She chose to fly with Gulf Air because she lived in Philly, and she wanted to be based at home. We would become better friends much later, but she was someone you knew you could trust. She could keep a secret, and she was always laid-back and hardworking.

A small charter airline had its drawbacks. We had a small fleet of older planes, and at any given time, when there was a mechanical malfunction of the aircraft or an irregular operation, we did not have backup aircraft. When there was a mechanical issue, the aircraft would remain grounded, very often at Caribbean outstations where there were no mechanics or replacement parts. Sometimes crews would be left sitting on the aircraft for hours, waiting for a part or mechanic to be flown in. The passengers would be left stranded until the aircraft was fixed, and sometimes it would be days, not hours. This began to happen with more frequency. The delays would be longer, the crews would become more frustrated, and the passengers angry before they even boarded. Sometimes the waits would be so long that the aircraft would be positioned off the airport tarmac, and the Flight Attendants would remove the overwing exit, get into their bikinis, and lay out on the wing. Huge safety no-no, but it was done.

Currently, I had been with Gulf Air for a year and seven months. I had made huge concessions and adjustments in my life to make it work. I began to realize this was a company that might be in trouble. There were more lengthy delays that happened with greater frequency. There were more Flight Attendant layoffs, and even pilots began to be furloughed.

I no longer had sightings of my former roommate or my clothes. There were rumors he was no longer with the company, but who knew or who cared? There had been rumors as well that some bills were not being paid by the company and that the airline was in financial trouble. We had all heard stories of airlines shutting down with no notice. It was rumored one airline crew received knocks on the doors of their layover hotels demanding payment for the room as non-payment of the company bills stacked up. Some crews were left stranded at outstations with no flights back to their home base. They had to rely on the generosity of other carriers who would fly them home for free or at a reduced rate. I did not want this to be me. Many of the Flight Attendants began to see the handwriting on the wall. The company was in trouble and might not last much longer.

It was around this time that most of the crew were demoralized and uncertain about the future of the company, and certainly about their own job security. Many of the Flight Attendants became no-shows or called in sick. I recall working with one of the Jersey girls, who had made it clear before departure that this would be her last flight. She was getting married (poor fellow) and would be leaving the sky behind. She grumbled about the company, the pay, and her flights, and her rant continued even as the passengers boarded. It was clear she would say and do whatever she felt. She worked the flight with a scowl on her face and barked at anyone who came in contact. I was behind her as we picked up meal trays and ran them back to the galley. She was carrying five meal trays, clearly annoyed when a passenger tugged on her apron. I saw her stop and give the passenger the fisheye as she tried to keep moving. Beef gravy was dripping down her apron. "Oh miss, could you bring me a blanket and a pillow? I asked for that twenty minutes ago." I saw as she continued to glare down at him. Then her response was loud and clear: "Certainly, sir, and if there is anything else, you can stick a broom up my ass, and I will sweep the aisle for you on the way back."

My commuter roommate had already given me notice that she was leaving the company. She said she had another offer with an airlink airline close to her home. We settled our obligations, and I wished her well. This left the responsibility of the apartment up to me. I felt the company would not last long enough to take on another roommate, so this left me with some tough decisions to make. My last few trips were surrounded by uncertainty and confusion. Sick calls and no-shows were happening more frequently. Most flights we worked were full, with only minimum crew, and then again, we were plagued with mechanical issues and delays with understandably angry passengers.

It was a tough decision to leave a company I had given up so much for to be a part of. I felt under the current circumstances that the situation was closing in, and it would be but a matter of time before I would find myself in a place I had no real connection to and without a job for which I had made so many concessions. It was bittersweet when I loaded my Jeep and drove away from Philly on a cold, windy, and snowy day. I did not know where I was headed, but I knew I still wanted to fly. I knew I might have been with the wrong company, but being a Flight Attendant was the right career for me. I still had time.

Chapter 6

Those Who Wander

I had no plans in mind when I left Philly. I knew I wanted to be back home for a while, plan a new strategy, most likely fall back into dentistry, and regroup my finances. Things looked grim when I thought about the decisions I faced. It would be good to see my family and friends, but it did not change the fact that I was taking myself with me once again, along with my decisions, problems, challenges, and feelings. My parents were concerned for me, of course. I pulled into their driveway on a Monday morning with no advance warning. They had many questions, which masked their concern for my future, but my mom always made me feel it would work out for the best. I would bide my time until I could get back in the air, but how? I would need to find a dental lab to make the most money as soon as possible, but where?

I reconnected with some of my dental colleagues back in Ft. Worth. I was given the phone number for a dental laboratory that was looking for a technician in New Orleans. My favorite town! It all happened quickly. I soon found myself a convenient dormer apartment in the French Quarter, just four blocks down from the cathedral. I started to feel alive again. I had a job at a lab uptown, and I was surrounded by history, food, and fun. I could lick my wounds, recoup my finances, and have a little fun as well. This would give me time to apply and possibly interview for another airline, hopefully a major carrier with an extensive international route system. It would take time, but time was now something I had.

My years living in the French Quarter broadened my horizons in several ways. I made new friends, partied my way through Mardi Gras, spent days in City Park and the New Orleans Museum of Art, and had many leisurely rides on the Uptown Streetcar through the Garden District. I saw the Pope ride by in his Popemobile from my fire escape dormer down Chartres Street during his first visit to New Orleans. This was also a time when the most critical and deadly days of the AIDS epidemic raged on. I lost many friends. The French Quarter experienced many deaths, as did the nation, before new drug cocktails became available.

This was also a time when most of the major airlines began to hire again. Flying domestically and internationally had begun to expand. Once again, I began the application process. I requested applications for airlines that matched my qualifications. I applied again to Continental in Houston. I felt it would be a good fit for me with its location and Flight Attendant bases, and I had learned more about them since my earlier application. I was also now experienced and hoped this might help me along in the process. I also applied to US Air in Pittsburgh and Northwest Airlines in Minneapolis.

My first interview was in Pittsburgh with US Air. I dressed in my conservative suit and dreaded tie and used the flight voucher I had received. It was a crowded group interview at a hotel near their headquarters. We were divided into groups and invited to introduce ourselves and tell a little about ourselves—where we were from, the work we had done, hobbies, and family. I was again nervous, and I cannot really explain why, except who can feel comfortable talking about themselves to strangers? Certainly, a well-thought-out strategy for airlines to ascertain who can easily relate to strangers.

The beautiful girl next to me was from Hattiesburg, Mississippi. She had an easy smile, and I could tell she was as nervous as I was, but we were able to give each other a smile in support after our turn to speak. They sent the group out of the room and told us we were to wait for our names to be called. If our names were not called, they thanked us for coming, and we would be free to leave. Her name was Margaret, and she was from Hattiesburg, she said as we sat next to one another, hoping our names would be called. She admitted her nerves, and we filled each other in on our experience and interview history. I confessed I had applied with all the airlines I could, and she had as well. We exchanged numbers for future reference and to stay connected as we both waited for the outcome.

We were both called back into the room in a semi-circle of six. They then called us into a room seated opposite a male and female interviewer. My nervousness was on full display, but I answered the questions as factually as possible. I tried not to fall into the trap of rambling. The interview ended; they thanked me for coming. They said I could expect a reply by mail within two weeks. I took a deep breath as I returned to the lobby to wait for the shuttle back to the airport.

I did not see Margaret again until I spotted her in the terminal. She was quietly waiting for her flight at the gate. She smiled when she saw me. "Oh, you have to connect in Memphis for your flight home!" I asked.

"Yeah, I won't be home until after nine tonight."

I asked how she felt it went for her. We both felt the same. It would be a waiting game, and it could go either way.

"Well, either way means yes or no, so I will try to think yes." She smiled.

I told her I would call if I heard anything, and I would stay in touch through the process.

"We will get hired, I am sure of it, but who knows when and with whom?"

Back in New Orleans, my mother informed me of someone from my past who felt the need to contact me. He had been a caregiver for a partner who had died and felt I was someone who would understand. We had been close in LA, and I did want to be there for him in this trying time. He had decided to move to Portland, but he was not the kind of person to ever be alone. He asked if I would come to visit or to live if I found Portland to my liking. Once again, I was on the move. I did caution him that I was applying to the airlines and hoped once again to fly. He was fully supportive.

He bought a house on the southeast side of Portland, and I moved in to help him get settled. I was thankful that I had all my airline mail sent to my mother's address so that nothing would be lost in the mail. She knew the importance of those applications for me, and she would let me know as soon as anything arrived. My first notification was from US Air. I asked my mother to read the letter to me.

US Air informed me I had not been selected for the Flight Attendant position and closed by inviting me to reapply in six months. I was disappointed, certainly, but I was not sure that this was the company for me. I called Margaret, and she had received the same letter. Turn-downs hurt, for sure, but hopefully, they would lead us to something better.

Portland was not a city I would have chosen to live in, and I could not see myself being there for a long time. It rained constantly, and it was cold for me, but it was verdant and green when the sun shined, but that did not happen often. I had indeed had enough overcast, cold, and rainy days in Philadelphia. The weather, coupled with the situation, was not only depressing, but the short days of sunlight often felt gloomy.

Always, there is an unseen benefit if one looks hard enough. Mine came in the form of a letter from Northwest Airlines. The airline would be hosting group interviews around the country, and I was invited to attend. The letter gave the minimum qualifications, and preference would be given to second-language speakers, with an emphasis on the Japanese language. Was I fluent in Japanese? No, but my thanks and gratitude go to the Japanese ladies I worked with in dentistry, who were my friends then, and they remain my friends now. These lovely women took the time and effort to teach me basic Japanese phrases, which hopefully, in this interview situation, would help. As luck would have it, there would be a group interview at the Sheraton Hotel at Portland Airport. This was great. The date was two weeks away, so it gave me time to prepare.

Northwest Airlines had a long history and legacy. It was one of the oldest airlines in the world. Started as a mail carrier with its bright red tail through the harsh winter conditions across the Great Plains and Minnesota, early flights through these conditions with poor visibility carried the mantra, "follow the red tail." After the war, it was Northwest Airlines that helped the Japanese in creating their own airline, and it was reported that Northwest Airlines Flight Attendants trained the flight crews who became Japan Airlines. Northwest Airlines had one of the earliest presences in Asia, and later the name became Northwest Orient Airlines. The airline was also one of the earliest airlines to fly the 747 aircraft, so they had a storied past and history, which I was later to learn more about.

The day of my interview, I arrived early at the hotel, and the lobby was already filling with well-groomed candidates of all ethnicities. This was exciting. I was nervous, but for inexplicable reasons, I felt more excited than nervous. All the candidates tried to mingle, to look relaxed, but as with these types of competitive interviews, who could truly relax? It looked to be a group of about fifty applicants. They opened the doors to the grand meeting room, and we filed in and took our seats. Every applicant appeared to be in conservative attire and impeccably groomed. The ones conducting the interview sessions appeared to be Northwest

Flight Attendants themselves. There were African American, Asian, Caucasian, Pacific Islander, and Indian American attendants there to interview us. This was the first interview session where I felt comfortable in the process.

As usual, one by one, we stood, introduced ourselves, and most gave a reason as to why they wanted to pursue the Flight Attendant position. After the group introduction, we were given information on a bit of company history and the company's hiring needs for the upcoming Asian expansion. We were then delegated into groups of twenty, and each group was paired off with a Flight Attendant recruiter.

"Would I be prepared to relocate? The Flight Attendant base openings were Honolulu, Los Angeles, and Detroit. Would those bases work for me? How soon could I start training if hired? I see you have worked as a Flight Attendant before. Why did you leave the company?"

All were questions I could respond to truthfully and with clarity.

"It says you have some knowledge of the Japanese language; can you speak for me?"

I spoke general phrases, and in my limited vocabulary, I stumbled through, but I did not—in retrospect—think the language portion of the interview was the strongest point. He was Japanese American and made me feel valued as a candidate. So many years later, having never had the chance to thank him personally, I never forget him or that day. He, without knowing, changed the trajectory of my life.

"If you have not received a phone call from us within seventy-two hours, it means we will not be going forward with your hiring. Is this the correct phone contact for you? Thank you for coming and for your interest in the Flight Attendant position with Northwest Airlines."

Early the next morning, I received the call. I would report for training at the Minneapolis training center to be a member of the training class of 1992.

Chapter 7

Dream Interrupted

As excited as I was about the possibility of training for this dream position, I was apprehensive about making my way through another six weeks of intense training. I had the feeling that training at the fourth-largest passenger airline in the world would be much tougher, more intense, and more demanding. Plus, as anyone who commits to this kind of career knows, it requires total commitment. It is not something that can be done in half measures. I learned with Gulf Air that one cannot let life get in the way of flying, but very often, flying might get in the way of life. I felt sad to be leaving Portland and the commitment I made there, but I was always upfront about the possibility that this might happen.

I arrived at the training facility adjacent to the Minneapolis-St. Paul International terminal with my luggage and new hire packet in hand. We were bused to apartment housing close to the airport. Six guys were assigned to a three-bedroom apartment. We quickly sized up who would share with whom. I knew that I would not have another roommate situation like I experienced with Gulf Air. These guys were all there for the same reason—to become part of Northwest Airlines. We quickly paired up, and I roomed with a Korean speaker who struck me as friendly but serious and well put together. We were a particularly good fit.

The following morning, we were outside for a 7:30 bus to take us to the F training building on the Northwest training campus. Fall was setting in to the Twin Cities, and the cold had already arrived. The bus drove past the massive hangar, which had a four-story graphic of a Northwest 747 aircraft. We would pass this daily going to and from the F building. That aircraft graphic was a daily reminder to us all of what we were about to become a part of. We were sent individually to a medical building just off the Northwest grounds for a company physical, along with sight and hearing tests. The F building had several floors, and there were many classrooms where other training classes were taking place. Our height and weight were measured, monitored, and noted. We were shuffled to many areas on the first couple of days of training, including taking photographs for our ID badges. These security badges were required every time we entered the building. They were the most important of all our required items.

Intensive classroom study began straightaway. There were several primary instructors. There was a tall, willowy Flight Attendant who had an easy smile, but she also gave one the feeling that she was not to be challenged in any way. She clearly made it known she was in charge, and I never knew for sure, but she was not a particular fan of the male new hires. Then there was the older, very senior Flight Attendant who oversaw the entire training program. There were male instructors as well, and we would get to know them all very well during these weeks of training. We received our indoctrination from the chief Flight Attendant. We had a curriculum package that we had received before arrival, which gave us the airport codes we needed to memorize. There were many. We were required to maintain at least an 82% proficiency on all tests. We could be cut from training at any given time for any infraction without question. Grooming, dress, and makeup were always monitored. Participation was encouraged, and it was noted if it appeared that your interest level was lacking. Classroom training began with the theory of flight and the company objectives. We were to be the face of the airline, and that meant we were to be well-trained and prepared for any emergency or situation.

The chilly early mornings, often in the dark, turned into long and demanding days, often returning to the apartment in the evening at dusk. We all supported and inspired one another. In the evenings in the apartment, we most often had classwork we needed to memorize—emergency commands, equipment location, or proper ways to handle emergencies.

At the end of my second week of training, we boarded the morning bus to the F building, and one of the girls boarded the bus in tears. She was at the top of the class as she aced every test. She was bright, beautiful, and caring. She supported everyone, and we collectively supported her.

"Oh my God, are you okay?" I asked as I sat in the seat behind her. The classmates filed on behind, and everyone looked concerned.

"I am being terminated," she said. "It seems all of a sudden I am a quarter inch too short."

All on the bus were shocked. All the questions were asked. Couldn't they measure again? Could she wear thicker socks? Certainly, she had exhausted all the questions. The company was adamant. Their height requirements were non-negotiable. She was on her way back home after receiving one hundred percent on all her exams.

Never could I have expected that my time was to come. Our classroom training continued. We also had a day of grooming where regulations regarding appearance were clearly dictated. The girls had a colorist who went over skin types, hair color, and makeup recommendations. The girls were given makeup kits and encouraged to try the recommended colors, which would work while wearing the uniform. The Honolulu girls all giggled and referred to one another as looking like Kabuki dancers. The guys were a bit off the hook, but hair length and facial hair would be strictly monitored. Also, no tattoos, rings, or piercings. I had scored well on my tests and hoped to continue. Midweek of our third week, we would begin our training in emergency equipment, commands, and procedures. The pressure was beginning to build. This was a time when we all became aware of those who were to be terminated. Any time an instructor would pull a candidate from a class, it would come with an instructor asking them to take their books and report to the head of inflight services.

I was in a morning class that was to begin emergency equipment training and location. In walked one of the male instructors. He came to me, confirmed I was David Edmondson, and he asked me to bring my books and proceed to the office of the head of inflight services.

"What? How could this be? What had I done or not done?"

I made my way down the second-floor hall and was told to take a seat, that she was with someone now. I was in a state of shock. There must be some mix-up, some confusion. Had I done something wrong? The door was opened just a crack, and I could hear someone in tears. She apparently was being let go. I could not hear the reasoning behind the situation, but through the sobs, I heard the girl ask if there would be a chance for her to reapply later. I heard the inflight supervisor slam her books onto the desk.

"Just look at these grades, look at your performance. Absolutely not. Do you think we would have you back after this? This is your pass for your flight back to your home. Good luck to you," she barked as she gestured toward the door.

The girl stumbled from the office, glanced in my direction, and hurried down the hall.

The head of inflight stood by the open door and appeared to have softened her stance. "You are David Edmondson," she asked casually. "Please come in. The reason you are here is that we have a situation that has come to our attention from the airline's medical clinic. It seems you have a medical situation that will require surgery to correct. You may not be aware of what is needed, but the clinic will provide you with what will need to be done to be in physical shape to return to training."

I sat momentarily speechless.

"Right, I had no idea there was any kind of a problem. So, I will be able to return to training when this is corrected, is that right?"

"Yes, your performance here has been excellent, and we would hate to see you go, so just get this taken care of, and give me a call at this number. After we receive a release from your doctor, we will assign you a new class date."

I was numb from shock as I sat in the middle seat on the flight back to Portland. Fortunately, leaving midday saved me from the embarrassment of having to make explanations or say goodbye to my roommates. It did not save me from the disappointment of the situation. I went over and over in my mind what had been discussed in that last meeting. I had the medical evaluation with me and what would be required to resolve the situation and get me back to training. My faith was at a low ebb, and I did not really see much hope in returning to training anytime soon. Once back home, I reconsidered my options.

Flying for this company was what I wanted to do, so I would have the corrective surgery and do whatever it would take to get me back there. In Portland, I had no doctor, no access to medical care whatsoever, and no health insurance to help with the payments. I quickly researched surgeons, scheduled appointments, itemized the cost, and decided to finance the surgery and what needed to be done. Within the week of being home, I was being prepped for outpatient surgery. Three weeks later, I was faxing the post-op results to the Northwest Airlines medical clinic, and I was free to reschedule a class date. The head of inflight was as good as her word (much to her credit in my eyes), and I was sent another new hire packet with a new class date. Yes, I would need to start training all over again, and ultimately, this process would end up costing almost two months of lost seniority, but I restarted training with the knowledge of what to expect going forward.

I arrived in Minneapolis in the dead of winter. The ground was blanketed with snow, and pockets of ice were everywhere. This class was being housed in different apartments in a nicer part of town located near a Byerly's Supermarket, which was iconic in Minneapolis. New roommates were sorted out, and the training started in the same way. The waits for the early morning bus to the F building were freezing cold; all the classmates had the same faraway look of anxiety on their faces. All were happy to be there, but not knowing what to expect. I chose to keep my having been here before a secret, as I felt it would not make a difference to anyone other than myself. It was a fresh start, and I wanted it to be that way. Once again, I went through the sight and hearing tests, the blood test, and the physical, which reconfirmed what I had been required to do from the original training. I went back to training with the full confidence that I would and could achieve my goal, this time with no distractions. New pictures and security badges were made, and I sailed through the early weeks with a feeling of déjà vu.

Picking up where I left off was with the emergency equipment location and use. The difference from my Gulf Air training was that Northwest Airlines flew a complete fleet of several different aircraft types, each with different emergency equipment and locations. We would need to memorize each and be tested on the operation and usage. Learning the in-depth emergency procedures required the knowledge of emergency commands, which could be different for each aircraft type. From the smallest aircraft in the fleet, the DC9-10, to the largest, the 747-400, emergency procedures differed greatly. The DC9 aircraft, which were some of the oldest in the Northwest fleet and were eventually phased out, were the original workhorses of the fleet early on. This plane had smaller seating capacity, the smallest with less than one hundred seats. This plane was built with two primary exits in the front of the plane and secondary exits overwing and the tail cone. In an emergency, the aft Flight Attendant would need to open an aft door connected to the aft jump seat, step through the tail cone while staying low and shouting the command "Stay Back" to keep from being rushed by passengers. Then the tail cone release handle would be pulled, causing the tail cone to drop. This ideally created a usable exit for the evacuation of the aft passengers. The emergency procedures on this aircraft required specific training and directives, which increased after the DC9-14 crash that was struck by a 727 in dense fog at Detroit airport on Dec. 3, 1990. The aft Flight Attendant who tried to jettison the tail cone was either rushed by passengers or the tail cone release failed. She died in the crash along with seven passengers.

In the future, I would fly this aircraft to smaller outstations such as Rochester, Minnesota, Minot, Traverse City, Lansing, or Flint. Some days in my reserve flying, I could fly up to five legs in a day with only thirty- or forty-minute flight times. I had an uneasy feeling about this aircraft and only flew these trips out of obligation, never by choice.

Most of the training was logical, made sense, and was easily absorbed. The overwater ditching procedures were anything but. In an emergency ditching in water, procedures were much more complicated. Ditchings, depending on aircraft type, would require door slides to become rafts. We were required to know which doors could be opened and the slides deployed (if the exit was not already underwater) and which slides were usable. Some slides might require repositioning at an exit that was still usable. We needed to know life vest operation, how to create a canopy, how to use flares and emergency location equipment, and when to release the raft from the aircraft. This remained a jumble of confusion for me, and I had many follow-up questions, but ultimately, I felt that in an actual ditching, your instinct would be the best directive.

Shouts of "Stay Back, Stay Back," or "Come This Way, Sit and Slide," or "Bend Over, Stay Down, Bend Over, Stay Down," could be heard from the training center. Sometimes at night, you could hear one of the roommates shouting this out in their sleep. It was such an intense environment—no release outlets, always tension-filled. We advanced to learning medical procedures and equipment, which for every Flight Attendant would at some point in their career be useful. Oxygen, CPR, defibrillators and their usage, low blood sugar, diabetic coma, heart attack, tourniquets, and even the procedures of birthing a baby. These procedures were very hands-on, and the knowledge and correct procedures could be lifesaving. We were required to go down an actual slide off a mockup of the 747. The slide was two stories from the ground or the pool, and as we gave the command "Sit and Slide," we each took our turn down the slide. We were told to dress casually for this drill, so I wore sneakers and jeans. When my turn came to go down the slide and I heard the command "Sit and Slide," I jumped onto the slide feet first. My sneakers caught on the slide, and I tumbled forward rather than going down on my backside. Fortunately, I was okay, but shaken a bit as I heard everyone gasp when I went over headfirst.

We continued to lose some trainees who were terminated or chose to drop out, unable to take the pressure or due to family concerns back home. At this point, those of us who had come this far anticipated graduation and becoming all for which we had trained. I began to be concerned about where my home would be after graduation. My friend in Portland decided the city and the weather were not a good fit for him. He accepted his old job back at Paramount Movie Studios in Hollywood. Beverly Hills was where we originally met in the seventies, so it would be back to LA for me after training. This was a good plan, as the bases that Northwest offered us as new hires were Detroit, Honolulu, or Los Angeles. Any base would do for me, but it was more realistic from a commuting standpoint to be home in LA. I was the fifth most senior in my class, so I felt I would receive my desired base selection. However, there was a caveat. The Flight Attendants who lived in Honolulu would receive the Honolulu base award superseding seniority. The Flight Attendant union later challenged this, but much too late to have had any effect on me. LA was my first choice for obvious reasons, so we waited for our base assignments to be announced.

Class 8 was one of the earliest classes to wear the new Disney-designed navy uniform. It was also the first class that was not issued both the old burgundy and fawn uniforms of the past and the new Disney design. Each Flight Attendant had their own feelings about the new uniform; I felt it was very well done. A simple blue suit for the guys with red and grey ties, skirts, and jackets for the girls, with newly simplified wings and name tags. We were measured and fitted for the uniforms, but first, we would need to complete the dreaded by some, and anxiously anticipated by others, supervised check rides.

My check ride took place on a bitter, frosty morning. It was an irregularly scheduled flight, a Minneapolis to Detroit turn on the 747. I was instructed to wear my own clothes—conservative slacks and a tie. It must have been a popular, easy day trip because it was crewed by a very senior group of Minneapolis ladies. I boarded the aircraft all smiles with the inflight supervisor, and I could feel the collective eye roll from these senior women. We were hastily introduced, and I was barked at about my bid position and was assigned to a jump seat. I did not have a clue as to what I was doing. I stowed my bag in the proximity of my assigned jump seat. The supervisor asked me to follow her as we inspected the emergency equipment in and around my assigned jump seat. She began to question me on the aircraft equipment locations—how many oxygen bottles were on board? How many halons? The senior Flight Attendants stood in the galley and seemed to be enjoying seeing me sweat. Now the passengers were boarding. It all seemed to happen so quickly. When I am in an uncomfortable situation and unsure of what I am supposed to do, I am sure I overcompensate by doing something—anything—that makes me feel useful. The seniors were instructed to have me do the service and for them to assist. The doors were armed by the senior, who had me watch the arming procedure. We were ready for takeoff. The supervisor took a passenger seat with clear visibility of my actions and responses. I followed the senior to the galley to set up the beverage cart, which I was told to work. The senior grabbed the cart and began stocking the top of the cart with cups, an ice bucket, lemons, and limes. I was told I was to work the cart, but the senior barked, "Just shadow me on the cart."

What did "shadow me on the cart" mean? So, I stood behind her looking rather foolish as the cart made its way down the aisle. I brought her fresh pots of coffee and tried to look like I belonged, but it was an unforgettable experience. I picked up trash, smiled when I could, and tried to look professional. Thank you, God, it was a short flight, and on the return, I relaxed knowing I knew a bit more of what I was doing. This check ride, however, was a gift. It was an eye-opening experience as to the duties and structure of fulfilling my expectations. I could only imagine what my fellow classmates were to experience on their own check rides. After hearing many of their stories, my check ride did not seem quite as bad in comparison.

Finally, graduation day arrived. This class of diverse personalities, opinions, hopes, and wishes achieved our collective goal. We each had our wings pinned on by the head of inflight services. We stood for our class picture and celebrated the moment. I thought about my original class and the weeks of training I went through only to have it so unexpectedly interrupted. This was a double victory for me. I was proud of myself that I did not give up on my dream. I had my wings; I would fly once again.

Chapter 8

Destination Detroit

We received our base assignments, and I was given my third choice, Detroit. I felt some of these assignments were given out of seniority order, especially with the directive that those from Honolulu would have the choice of being based there. I was skeptical of the fairness of this process, but I would not be making waves as a new hire. Again, I practiced acceptance and began to think about how I could make a commute to Detroit work. It would require a commuter hotel and depend on my schedule of reserve days to make things work. As a new hire reserve Flight Attendant, I would be required to be within 90 minutes of my base, ready to be called out at any time, and able to get to the airport within that time. I felt it would be impossible to make it back to LA with only one or two days off, so I decided to take a commuter room.

I was still uncomfortable with roommate situations, having dealt with the trauma at Gulf Air and having just come off collectively nine weeks of shared living, so I pulled out the plastic and took a room at one of the airport hotels. I was unaware at the time of the dark history of my Detroit airport hotel. On February 17, 1991, Nancy Ludwig, a Minneapolis-based Northwest Flight Attendant, was brutally raped and murdered in a second-floor corner room near the back stairwell exit. It took months for the crime to be solved. Jeffrey Gorton, a serial killer and sexual deviant, killed her. This murder later changed several security measures involving Flight Attendant layover safety and security.

My first few days on call, I remained close to the phone. This was a time before cell phones, so I relied on the hotel phone or on my pager. You could not miss a call from crew scheduling, or you would be considered a no-show, which was grounds for termination. I flew with several of my classmates who were also assigned to the Detroit base. Most were trying to adjust with commuter rooms, commuting, working short call flights, and trying to stay legal with all the rules and regulations we were required to follow.

My first trips were uneventful; most were DC9 trips with several boardings daily. They helped me ease into the service flow and pick up speed on my service delivery. I had gotten rusty from my years away from the 727 flying with Gulf Air, and service there was never off beverage carts, only run-off twelve-cup tray carriers. We flew out of the old Detroit Metro Airport, but there was a new airport to be built, which was to be for Northwest Airlines specifically, but that was to come later. At this time, we could put in for a base transfer. As soon as your base of choice had an opening and your seniority could hold it, you would be awarded that base transfer. I felt lucky indeed. After three months of flying out of the Detroit base, I was awarded my transfer to LA. Things were looking up.

Back in LA, I set out to find an apartment that would be affordable for both of us. My friend had settled into the legal department at Paramount, and we both needed an apartment that would be more permanent and affordable. He was an expert at this, so I went along with whatever he decided. It happened to be a high-rise in the Hollywood Hills. A bit of a drive to LAX, but within the legal limit of flying. I was still on reserve, but I would experience a whole new world of flying. The LA base had some domestic flying, but the international flying was much more exciting. There were flights to Tokyo, Seoul, Honolulu, Sydney, Guam, and points in Southeast Asia, which were done through the Tokyo Flight Attendant base. Northwest was still the largest American airline to Asia.

Chapter 9

La La Land

Any job that requires image and visibility is often highly judged and scrutinized. This is always the case regarding the Flight Attendant position. Flight Attendants are the face of the company they represent. That perception may have changed over the years, but the reality remains the same. Like actors or film stars, Flight Attendants often play a part that requires them to act. They must smile through anger or challenge, appear energetic when they are exhausted, and remain civil and diplomatic when they are ready to implode. That is acting! Acting is only part of the equation; they are often required to become nurses in medical emergencies, crisis managers, diplomats, guards, service providers, and, most importantly, safety professionals. We are there to save your lives if necessary, and all else comes secondary. Over time, like film stars, male or female Flight Attendants have created the ultimate faux pas: they have aged, their hair is greyer, their waistlines have expanded, and their attitudes about the job have changed as well. Do keep in mind the catch-22 of the position: your position and value only increase with your years of doing the job. Seniority is everything. Of course, this is all relative. There are thirty-year Flight Attendants who perceive themselves as junior, and certainly, they are, comparatively speaking, to the ones more senior. There may also be a six-year Flight Attendant who perceives themselves as senior, and they are as well, to those hired after them, and for some who may still be on reserve or considered new hires.

The LA base certainly had a unique group of personalities. From senior to junior, the Flight Attendants at the LA base lived up to the image of the city and the myth. Many were young and beautiful. Many were aspiring models or actors, former beauty queens, bodybuilders, or in the porn industry in their off time.

My first trips out of the LA base were often short call-outs to Tokyo or Osaka. It was a fast learning curve to get up to speed on these international flights. They were usually a mix of very senior or very junior Flight Attendants. Usually, the junior call-outs were filling in for sick calls or rerouting. In an ordinary check-in, we were required to make a 2-to-8-hour phone check-in and then a 2-hour sign-in at inflight at the airport. Being on reserve, the 2-to-8-hour call was often waived, as I was well within that time limit of the call-out. Often, I could reach the aircraft when the door was being closed. This meant scrambling for my jump seat and work position, but the benefit of such close calls was that the boarding was complete. I would wipe the perspiration off my brow and take my place at the video screen for the safety demo. There were several times when I worked an Asia trip that I would be deferred to the lead Flight Attendant position, which required a multitude of extra responsibilities. The lead had to brief the cockpit crew, give a Flight Attendant briefing to the Flight Attendants, make announcements, handle the spill (the paperwork listing all passengers, crew, and flight stats), schedule crew breaks, and handle duty-free money and paperwork. Most often, these flights were on the 747-400 aircraft, with a capacity of 404 passengers on two levels.

Most Asia flights I would work in the aft cabin economy, which at this time was in the last gasp (pardon the pun) of smoking. It always seemed to be the case that the seniors who were smokers were always bidding first class and upper deck. As an adamant non-smoker, I found myself on the door four jump seat choking on smoke in the smoking section. Often, during the movie, I would find the seniors who smoked sitting on my jump seat puffing away.

My first months at the LA base were not only a practical learning experience but a social and cultural one as well. These were still times when the HIV-AIDS epidemic was adapting to medications and innovations, but for some, this was too late in coming. We had a working Flight Attendant at the LA base who was in the last stages of AIDS, with visible signs of the ravages on his face and hands. I flew two trips with him, and while personally nice, I could tell he was angry and very bitter about his situation and the way the company was handling him. He unloaded his feelings to me in the galley on one of the trips we flew together. The company had suggested he take a desk job where he would not be scrutinized by the passengers and, from their point of view, not made to feel uncomfortable. In his anger, he rebelled and tried to make a legal case that they were trying to deny him his right to perform the job he was hired and trained to do. While this was a sticking point for him in his anger and rage, he acted in sometimes inexplicable ways to get the company to fire him. In his thinking, he could take legal action. Some of his actions included leaving his crew linens in the crew bunk after his break, and at one time, I walked into the mid-galley, and he had placed his upper denture on a towel on the galley counter. Most crew members that flew with him fell into the categories of outrage or compassion. It was shortly after my last flight with him that I saw the notification in inflight. He had peacefully passed away.

My first Christmas, still on reserve call-out at the LA base, found me called out for a military charter to the military base of Yokota near Tokyo. I was deferred as lead on this flight, and there were many unique rules and regulations that were enforced by the commanding officer in charge. We had unique safety regulations for these kinds of charters as well. Gun stowage, seating, and meal service all had set parameters. Once boarded, the flights were easy to work; the service members were very disciplined, polite, and a joy to serve.

On arrival, it was in our Flight Attendant contract that we had to be housed at the best hotel around the arriving airport. I am not sure that the contract committee had paid a visit to this hotel, but the crew bus took the flight crew to what appeared to be some sort of Japanese inn. The rooms were dark, and the beds were low to the floor, with a small television with several Japanese channels only. We arrived on Christmas Eve, and most of the crew had been called out on this trip, most likely due to sick calls or call-offs because of Christmas. One sweet member of the flight crew had brought small individually wrapped gifts for each of the Flight Attendants. She was the bright spot of the crew, but there was no clever way to put lipstick on this pig of a layover.

I have always been a foodie. It has always been my thought that if I had decent food, I could make anything work. I was exhausted after the long flight, and our arrival had been after meal hours. The restaurant downstairs looked as though it was an afterthought. All I could see was a Japanese lady with a head covering stirring a pot, but the restaurant was not open. I inquired at the front desk, and I was directed to an actual 7-Eleven take-out store. It was about a quarter-mile walk to the store, which stocked mostly dry noodles and Japanese snacks and candies. I bought what I could and returned to my room and the lumpy mattress close to the floor.

I woke up early on Christmas morning with thoughts of Christmas Day back in LA. Thoughts of food at Cantor's Deli or Johnny's Steak House, and thoughts of my family back in Texas. This Christmas would pass me by. I headed down to the restaurant, which was, in fact, open, but I was the only one there. Always a bad sign. A Japanese lady appeared to take my order as I begged for coffee, not tea. I relished the seafood tempura and the bowl of rice, as something at least was cooked. The restaurant had a full wall of glass that looked out onto grassy fields adjacent to railroad tracks. I was preparing to pay my bill when I felt all hell break loose. The walls shook, the glass creaked, and dishes bounced around the table. At first, I thought a train had rumbled by. I looked at the lady working in the restaurant. She gestured with her hands, indicating an earthquake. It happened so quickly, and the aftershocks continued until the crew bus picked us up for the return flight from Yokota. This would be a true test of earthquakes to experience in the future. This was the first of several miserable Christmases I would spend while flying.

As the LA base continued to expand, new and junior Flight Attendants continued to transfer in. I became friendly with a new hire from Seattle who had left a settled lifestyle with a husband and five kids to follow her dream to fly. She was attractive, friendly, and easy to get to know. She was also desperate for a commuter place as she was sitting on reserve. She approached me about crashing at my apartment. I would need to run it past my partner. She was happy to pay whatever was needed, and I thought the extra income might help subsidize our expenses. She would not be in the apartment much, as the reserve call-outs were frequent. My partner was very much against the whole idea but reluctantly agreed to a trial run. It was made clear to her that if for any reason it did not work out, she would need to find another place—no harm, no foul.

There was a great deal going on with this girl. Yes, she had followed her dream, but her marriage and family were being put to the test in the process. In her first month of flying from the LA base, she was assigned the seven-day Sydney-Osaka trip, which was one of the most senior trips in the system. On this trip, she hooked up with a first officer. He was younger than she was, and later, to be filled in on the details, he was extraordinary at sex. She was madly in love. She talked as if she were planning a life with him, but there seemed to be no consideration about her life back in Seattle. She tried to be available to him, but as he was a pilot on reserve, it was difficult. She called one day when I was on my days off. Could she bring him to the apartment? He was due to fly out the following day, and they would truly have little time to be together.

My partner was at work, so I really had no way to let him know they would be using the bedroom for the night. I tried to sleep that night, but the smell of her perfume, coupled with the yelps, screams, and groans coming from that bedroom, was more than human flesh could endure. Certainly, there was no judgment on my part. Good for her; she was in love and living her dreams. I just wanted to get some sleep and have a modicum of peace while I was on my days off. My partner put his foot down.

"No more," he said. "She has got to go."

I was in reluctant agreement. She then decided to commute back to Seattle and hotel it, I assume. I never knew what happened to her as I did not see her again. I assume she changed bases, reconsidered the situation with her family, or had had her fun and was ready to return to her former life. We were each living our own reality.

One of the many personalities that flew out of this base was a drop-dead handsome male FA. He was gay and had a lively, fun, and humorous personality with absolutely no ego. His looks were a combination of a young Don Johnson and Rob Lowe. I often smiled when I would watch the passengers follow his every move as he moved through the cabin. Flight Attendants, both male and female, loved him. As with most physically beautiful people, there is always the reality of what their looks would bring to them. My conversations with him were always telling and at times disturbing. He lived just below my apartment in the Hollywood Hills. We had some frank jump seat conversations, mostly in whispered voices, as had the passengers overheard them, some would have been outraged. He had capitalized on his youth and beauty in several ways early on before he became a Flight Attendant. He had modeled, and he had been a boy cage dancer who dropped from the ceiling at the hugely popular gay disco, Studio One, in West Hollywood. At this time, he was in a long-term and very troubled relationship with a former LAPD officer. He filled me in on the details of his life. This was a revelation about my perceptions of others. His looks would have you believe he lived a charmed life, but there was so much in his real life that was dark and disturbing. He was in a dangerous and physically abusive relationship. His partner would often drink and use him as a punching bag. I expect he would need to exhaust his sick calls just to recover from the black eyes or broken ribs. He related to me that in one violent confrontation, his partner had tried to pull out his hair with pliers. After he tried to leave this maniac, all the windows were broken out of his BMW, and all the tires were flattened. What does one say to someone who has gone through trauma like this? I have never had tolerance for violence of any sort, having experienced this at an early age as I was forced to watch this happen to my mother. This was the nineties, however, and how could this still be happening? It was much later, and after a base change for us both, when I came into contact with him once again. He was still handsome, still smiling, but there was a sadness around the eyes. Something had changed. I later learned he was battling a progressive type of cancer. It was four months later that I was shocked to see his obituary in Detroit inflight. Yet another candle in the wind!

Models, actors, comics, and beauty queens were all a part of the LA base. I flew some domestic patterns. As my seniority grew, I held a line, which was a gift after all the time sitting on reserve waiting for call-outs. I flew with a sweet and beautiful FA who was a former beauty queen. This was a time I chose to take my mother on a trip to Hawaii. We were fortunate to be upgraded to first class on the DC 10 aircraft. We were fortunate that this beautiful girl was working lead and first class. My mother, who never met a stranger, felt the need to stop the Flight Attendant to tell her how beautiful she was.

"Hon, you could be a beauty queen," my mother said adamantly.

The Flight Attendant smiled demurely.

"Actually, I was," she said shyly. "I was Miss New Mexico, but I can't fall back on that much longer," she chuckled as she picked up our drink glasses.

She later became the Flight Attendant with her arms fully extended as if she was flying through the air in her Northwest uniform. This was on the giant billboard, which was seen as you entered LAX with the new Northwest ad campaign: "SOME PEOPLE JUST KNOW HOW TO FLY."

At this time, when I flew internationally, it was to Tokyo or Asia on a 747 aircraft. I did some Honolulu trips as well, mostly flying the DC 10. My seniority was improving as new hires were continuing to be trained. The Tokyo trips were long and tiring, but in most aspects easier to work than some. The Japanese passengers were a dream to board on most any flight. They traveled light; they found their seats and buckled up with little confusion or fuss. Asia was a competitive market for all airlines, and Northwest still had a larger footprint with its network there. We were required to maintain high service standards to Japan, especially in first and business cabins. The Japanese economy was the strongest in the world at the time, and most flights were full. These were mostly crewed with senior Flight Attendants.

Our layover hotel at Tokyo's Narita Airport was a luxury high-rise near the airport. This hotel housed primarily Northwest crews and was booked to capacity daily. Sometimes there would be a wait for a room, which required sitting in the lobby. After a twelve-hour demanding flight, it was easy to nod off while waiting. Of course, this was a faux pas, as crews were never to be seen sleeping in uniform. When you are tired, you are tired, so we did our best not to snore or drool. Our crew reached the hotel one overcast afternoon, and we were told there would be a long wait for rooms. Apparently, one of the earlier South Fly flights was canceled, so the rooms were not turning over as fast as usual. I only hoped that the hotel was not oversold, and they would not need to bus us to the spillover hotel. I did not want to even think about that. It was a lengthy wait in the lobby, and they began to call our names for us to claim our room keys. I got a room number I was not familiar with and was in no mood to stumble through the hallways looking for my room. The concierge informed me that I was given one of the basement rooms. These rooms had a reputation of being the least desirable, as they were beautifully done but had no windows, and were dark and cold as well. "That is simply great," I thought as I punched the elevator to zero. I made my way to the room, opened the door to the damp and musty smell of the basement, and threw my bags on the floor. I was exhausted and hungry. I pulled a chocolate bar out of my bag, took a couple of bites, and sat on the bed. I set the half-eaten candy bar on the nightstand and lay across the bed. The next thing I remember is the noise of chewing and the rattling of paper. I woke up, and in the lamplight, I could see a huge rat gnawing away at my candy bar. I must have yelped or shouted, but whatever I did sent the rodent scurrying. Still half asleep and partially comatose, I thought I was trapped in a nightmare. I called the front desk and tried to remain calm, but I was clearly done in. In my broken Japanese, I begged for a change of rooms, but the hotel was full. I was out of options. The front desk said they would send someone down, and my thinking was, "What in hell could anyone do? Chase the rat, set up a cage?" I laid back across the bed and must have fallen asleep. The sound of the doorbell woke me. I went to the door and peered through the peephole before opening the door. I opened the door to two Japanese hotel employees dressed in full hazmat suits holding a broom, a bucket, and a dustpan. If I had not been so tired, this would have been laughable. I repeated, "Nezumi" (rat) had "Kieru" (disappeared). The rat had disappeared. They looked under and behind the bed. "Gomennasai," they repeated. All I wanted was to go to sleep. I turned the heat on full blast as they left, bowing with apologies.

Most crews that worked the Tokyo flights from all bases found their groove at the layover hotel. Crews that bid these flights regularly had a set routine. They would arrive at the hotel, nap for a couple of hours, and head down to a restaurant called The Yellow Awning. They would then begin a night of eating and drinking, mostly drinking until they reached the eight hours before flight rule, which was a mandatory cutoff time for drinking before a flight. The dining was Japanese style, shoes off and sitting on the floor, which I never found comfortable or appealing. I was never a big drinker or one who liked to socialize with the crews. Nothing against that, but for me, I felt I had had enough of the crew while working on such long flights. I preferred to explore the areas and be out and about with the people. This hotel had a wonderful buffet of both Japanese and Western dishes, and I always enjoyed a breakfast with Japanese salad, rice, and eggs.

Working the long-haul international routes, while rewarding, could also be challenging. The biggest challenge for me was duty-free sales. It was inexplicable to me that most international passengers would have an unlimited selection of items to buy at any duty-free store inside every international airport, but no. We had to run carts down the aisle and interrupt the passengers' movies while we sashayed down the aisle waving a duty-free catalogue like some street vendor. It was required, and it was done, but for me, it was some kind of misery. We had to pre-inventory the carts before the sales began, and we had to do a closing inventory after the sales, lock and seal the carts for landing, and pray that it all balanced out in the process. We sold a collection of goods, from perfume to tobacco to chocolates to jewelry to watches. Some items could run into the thousands of dollars. We were required to sell any item in any monetary currency. It was a nightmare. We would sell a five-hundred-dollar watch in US dollars, an expensive necklace in Thai baht, and a twelve-dollar box of candy in Japanese yen. The cabins were dark because of the movies, so we carried our flashlights. The currency all looked the same in such poor lighting, and the Queen was on every kind of currency. Even with the currency conversion charts, I never quite knew for sure if my count would balance out. We were also required to have our currency and paperwork in order to turn in to the lead Flight Attendant before the second service prior to landing.

Chapter 10

Wonder Down Under

The Sydney-Osaka trips were considered the most desirable in the system. These trips were seven-day patterns worth the most flight times in a schedule. They also included great layovers in luxury hotels, excellent food, and wonderful excursions.

Another personality that flew out of the LA base at this time was a beautiful girl who was also a model and centerfold in several of the leading men's magazines. It was said the company did not take issue with her sideline career as long as she never appeared in photos wearing any part of the Northwest uniform. While beautiful, she did have quite a mouth, and expletives could roll off her tongue easily. I found myself working my first Sydney-Osaka seven-day trip with this girl and several more interesting crew members, along with a couple of my classmates. These trips were long, fourteen-hour exhausting flights with crew breaks factored in because of the extended flight times. At this time, we still had the full seven-cart China service with caviar served from ice molds in the first-class cabin. There was also a mid-movie high tea in first class as well. The seats did not fully recline, but almost. In first and business class on the 747-400, the FAs working these cabins were required to wear the uniform-issued grey serving jacket, which set them apart from the economy cabins.

On these flights, and in any class of service, alcohol consumption was a given. While the sale of alcohol in the main cabin generated much-needed revenue for the company, it was a catch-22 as alcohol consumption generated many of the onboard problems during the flight. I was still on reserve call-out for this flight as it departed during the Christmas holidays, which would mean we would be spending Christmas Eve and Christmas Day in Sydney. It was summer down under, so we were all looking forward to an Aussie Christmas. Predictably, the junior crew was delegated to the smoking section in the aft coach cabin. I was also required to assist with pre-departure drinks on the upper deck before takeoff. We would open several bottles of wine, serve the champagne, and stow the pre-departure items in preparation for takeoff. Every seat was taken. We all looked forward to the fourteen hours passing quickly and without incident.

It was a lively group of passengers, and with the meal service over, it was time for the dreaded duty-free sales during the movie. We finished the cart inventory and made our way toward the mid-galley, flashlights in hand. As my back was to the galley, I heard shouting in the aisle. As I turned, I could see two male passengers throwing punches at one another. I tried to move down the aisle to diffuse the situation, and at the same time, a Flight Attendant who was in the galley heard the disruption and was behind the man in the aisle. At this point, the younger man threw another punch, which missed and struck the Flight Attendant squarely in the face. That section of the cabin erupted as the other FAs called the lead to report the incident to the captain. When the punch hit the Flight Attendant, the situation escalated to interfering with a flight crew member. The relief pilots came back and subdued the passengers, who happened to be father and son going home for Christmas. The Flight Attendant who was struck certainly had her Christmas and trip ruined. She would have facial bruising for the entire trip.

We arrived at the glorious Wentworth Hotel early in the morning. This hotel was a grand and luxurious hotel in downtown Sydney, close to Circular Quay, the ferry port, shopping, and the Grand Centennial Park. The hotel, originally built as a layover hotel for the Qantas flight crews in the sixties, had a lovely Australian woman as its concierge, and the flight crews loved her. She had each room key ready and was waiting for a very exhausted crew who was happy to see her. My room was unforgettable. It was a corner room, all marble, with a sweeping view of downtown Sydney and the Harbour Bridge. I could see the Aussie flag waving in the wind atop the bridge. It was a clear and sparkling summer day. My only thought was to shower and sleep. I peeled off my uniform to hang in the closet. It reeked of cigarette smoke and aircraft. I tightly closed the closet door, but that did not help. The smell seeping off that uniform would keep me awake, even as exhausted as I was. It would have to be sent to the cleaners downstairs. After a shower, I lay across the bed but was too wired to sleep. I got up and decided to take a walk in the warm, fresh air. I walked into the park and made my way past the Sydney Tower and the magnificent shopping mall. Having familiarized myself with the area around the hotel, I returned to the room for some sleep. I had this day to myself, but the whole crew would be going to the beach at Manly tomorrow. I may not be a beach person, but this was an Australian beach considered to be one of the best in the world.

We met in the lobby to go as a group. We took the ferry from Circular Quay to Manly, cruising past the Opera House and the Harbour Bridge. It was Christmas Day down under. What a beautiful day it was. Manly is a quaint little seaside town that gives one the feeling of being in an ethereal place. The shops and houses were brightly painted, and the streets at the ferry landing were lined with small, tidy shops. There were ice cream vendors on the street. We found a stretch of beach, and some in the group laid out our towels while others headed for the surf. I joined the group in the water, which was crystal clear, and began to enjoy myself. In the water, I struck up a conversation with one of the girls. It turned out she had been in the afternoon group of my class. This was my connection to Clare, who would later become my confidant, voice of reason, laughter and fun, and, best of all, my friend.

Our day at the beach gave some of us a little too much sun. Our centerfold relished being topless as the day wound down. I took an earlier ferry back to Darling Harbour to have an early dinner and rest up. We had tickets for a Christmas concert at the Sydney Opera House, which I did not want to miss.

The next morning, I went downstairs at the hotel where there was a lavish buffet breakfast being served. I was early, and most of my crew was still recovering from late-night drinks at the bar and the Sydney nightlife. I noticed a woman seated at the next table. She smiled and acknowledged my presence. I was still waking up, so I hoped she would not require conversation as I sipped my coffee.

"Are you enjoying your stay?" she asked.

I looked around. Yes, she was talking to me.

"Yes, very much," I smiled, "and you?"

"Oh, I have been here for a couple of months now," she replied.

Did I hear her correctly, a couple of months? She happily went on to fill me in on her two-month stay. I listened intently as her story unfolded. It sounded like something straight out of *Days of Our Lives*.

She was a Flight Attendant as well, with another American carrier. She was working a flight from San Francisco to Sydney. Her departure was indeed two months ago. As the 747 began its descent into Sydney Airport, she felt something pop around her eyes. She said she felt a bit dizzy but thought nothing of it until she made it through customs and onto the crew bus. By the time she reached the hotel, she had a blinding headache.

"All I could think about was getting to my room to lie down," she continued. "I laid across the bed and went into a deep sleep." She still had the headache, but when she woke, her pillows and sheets were covered in blood. She called the front desk, and they rushed an ambulance, which took her to the hospital. It was explained to her that on descent, the change of pressure in the cabin had caused an opening from her brain into the sinus cavity.

"Wow," I said. "I don't think I have ever heard of such a thing."

"Neither had I or the doctors who treated me," she said.

My next question was why she was not home for further treatment. Apparently, she had been told by the doctors that she could not fly due to the possibility that this could happen to her again. I asked her how she was able to pay the bills at such a luxury hotel for so long.

"Oh, the company is paying her bills. She will need to stay at the hotel until they can find a boat to get her home."

When asked if she was not homesick or missed her family, she shrugged and said she had divorced her husband back in Houston and had put everything she owned in storage. I got the feeling this was not the first time she had related this story to anyone who would listen. It appeared to me she might be at this hotel as long as the insurance held out. Interestingly, however, I never saw her again on my subsequent Sydney trips.

The Osaka portion of the trip was a couple of hours shorter flight time, but certainly demanding. We had a wonderful layover hotel that was always accommodating to the NWA crews. The hotel was located in downtown Osaka, which I could never quite figure out where downtown started and ended. It was as if it were one mega city as far as the eye could see. There was a convergence of crews from all bases that would get together in a ballroom allocated for crew. We would drink, party, dance, and have a wonderful time merging and meeting up with other bases and crews. Eventually, all crews would get thrown out of this hotel due to the wild partying that went on. All bases received a notification of conduct to crews that this hotel had been taken off the crew hotel list for trashed rooms, loud music, and Flight Attendants doing yoga in their pajamas in the lobby. When challenged about the yoga situation, the FA's response was that her room was too small. There had also been reports of soba noodles in the swimming pool and other unacceptable behavior. On my next Osaka trip, I did find our crews in a different hotel.

Chapter 11

Emerald Buddha

My partner and I talked about using my passes to take a long-overdue leisure trip. We traveled well together, and we both had a desire to see Bangkok. We had seen too many reruns of *The King and I* and wanted to experience the real deal. We used my passes from LAX to Tokyo Narita, connecting on to Bangkok. We were upgraded to business, so it was a luxurious trip with a wonderful Asian South Fly crew. Crews out of the Tokyo base were made up of all Asian nationals, with the contractual exception that the lead FA position had to be American. The lead who bid this trip gave us helpful tips on where to eat, drink, and visit.

We checked in to the Intercontinental Bangkok Hotel. This hotel was originally built for the Pan Am crews when Pan Am still owned the hotel chain. Exotic is the best way to express the opulence of this hotel—fresh fruit in the rooms, peacocks on the lawn, and beautiful macaws in cages. It was otherworldly. There was so much to do and see. We set out to see the Royal Palace, which was actually the king's residence—a city of gold. These grounds housed the sacred Temple of the Emerald Buddha. This visit to the Royal Palace and the Temple of the Emerald Buddha, the most sacred temple in all of Thailand, left me in jaw-dropping awe. Coming from a tiny town in North Texas, I could never have imagined the magnificence of such a place. I did not want to leave. I would return many times over the years just to savor the feeling of being in such a sacred and spiritual place.

Bangkok, being a city of water, is dominated by the mighty Chao Phraya River and its estuaries. Much like Venice, the city required hiring boats to navigate. The boats themselves were intricately carved and golden. We hired a boat that took us to the Royal Barge Museum, which housed the magnificent barges used by Thai royalty. We then hired a tuk-tuk, an actual motorcycle with a passenger seat and canopy, which could be hired very cheaply to take us to the Jim Thompson House, located in a residential area on a small and secluded estuary of the river. We felt as if we had taken our lives into our hands as the vehicle darted in and out of traffic. We choked on car exhaust and pollution, enhanced by the heat and humidity.

The Jim Thompson House is considered iconic and mythical in Thai culture, sacred to the Thai people. Jim Thompson was an American businessman with a love for the Thai people and Thai history. He is credited with reviving the Thai silk industry, and at this location, he began his collection of Thai and Asian art, amassing the largest collection of historical Thai, Laotian, and Burmese art, structures, and architecture in the nation. Thompson mysteriously disappeared in the jungles of Malaysia in 1967.

Upon arrival at the Jim Thompson House, we were unprepared for the absolutely overwhelming stench emanating from the water. The rivers and waters that ran through the city had suffered from years of pollution, dumping, and raw sewage. In other parts of the city, where the waters flowed, the stench wasn't as bad, but here, the water had no movement, and the air was almost too putrid to breathe. As we held handkerchiefs to our noses, this was yet another place of endless history and treasures not to be missed.

Bangkok was my first real taste of cultural awareness. The lives of the people were so different from our own. Here were people who lived day to day in a way that was all they knew and all they had come to accept, yet they were a smiling, gentle people. They seemed to have no judgment, only grace and beauty, yet that grace came into conflict when you ventured to areas like Patpong and the red-light district, where underage girls and boys were prostituted and sold. Awareness would come to me in many forms, often in stark contrast to logical thinking.

On our walk back to the hotel, it was a sweltering ninety-degree day. We came to a small pedestrian bridge, which we crossed, but in the center of the bridge, I noticed an object laid on a ragged cloth in the direct sun. As I looked down, I saw what appeared to be an armless and legless figure, a human torso. As I looked down, the figure looked into my eyes. I became overwhelmed with rage and feelings I had never experienced before. My first instinct was to look away, but I forced myself to look. I wanted to be aware of how shameful humanity can sometimes be. I noticed the beggar's cup prominently placed next to the torso. How could it be that someone who would never be able to care for himself was used in such a way? I searched the crowd for the person responsible for this exploitation. I saw no one, and even if I did, what could I do? If I put money in that cup, it would not help this person; it would only allow his keeper to continue to use him in this way. All I could do was cry. My friend pulled at my arm. "There is nothing you can do, David. Let it go," he said. I left that bridge and walked back to the hotel, but this was something I would never be able to "let go."

On our last day at the hotel, we sat by the pool, watching the peacocks on the manicured lawns and looking up at the blue sky. The blue of the sky was somewhat diminished by the haze of smog and humidity, but it was still there. As I looked up at the coconut palms, I could see silver metal bands at the top of the trees, just under the palm fronds. Each palm tree had these. I was curious, so I asked the cabana boy what they were for. He explained that they were metal bands to prevent the rats from climbing into the palm fronds and nesting. Clever, I thought, but not all the rats are in the trees!

Spirituality in the East is somewhat in conflict with Western spirituality. Certainly, spirituality is far different from religion, at least for me. Whether it's religion or spirituality, it doesn't give people the right to judge others based on their own reality. There will always be those who have and those who have not. Is this where karma comes into play? Why is one person given so much while another is given so little, and who ultimately decides? I have always been drawn to people and places where people live the life they were given, finding joy in what comes to them, rather than from those who can buy the life they think they deserve. Bangkok changed me in many ways. I would always find a way to return.

Chapter 12

One of the Guys

After graduation, and for most new-hire Flight Attendants, the drive and motivation to be the best is always the focus. It is hard to perceive that we have become but one cog in a wheel of literally thousands who do this job in any given company. How is it possible to be better, or even to be perceived as better, when we are all in the same uniform and perform the same repetitive task every flight? I never thought it possible until I met Michael.

We both ended up based in LA. Michael was from the upper Midwest, and to meet him was to know him, or want to know him better. He had an easy smile, a gentle nature, and passengers and crew alike loved him. We shared a similar sense of humor, which I am always drawn to, and a strong work ethic.

We were assigned a seven-day Sydney-Osaka. This was a crew around the same seniority, which enabled us to choose our bid positions and allowed us to work together. It was at the hotel in Sydney that Michael and I set out for a day together walking the park, going up in the Sydney Tower, and strolling the mall. Michael, with his sunny disposition, seemed lit by the sun. On the Osaka flight, three of us bid for the Business Class cabin on the main deck. At this time, Northwest had revamped the cabin options, which did away with the full-class cart services and became all Business Class on all aircraft. This was still a premium service but much more streamlined. We laughed and bantered the entire flight. We were working with another Flight Attendant who had a similar sense of humor, and we had way too much fun. We made our layover plans for Osaka, and I was excited to spend another day with such fun guys.

We agreed to meet in the lobby and go for the breakfast buffet, which always gave us a generous crew discount. The Japanese Yen was at an all-time high in those days, so every little bit helped on our layovers. Michael and I met in the lobby at the appointed time, but the other FA was a no-show. That seemed a bit odd in light of the fact that it was *his* plan for us to meet. Michael and I discussed what we should do. We didn't want to proceed without him, and we had his room number. We decided to go up and check with him to see what he would like us to do.

We reached his room and knocked but got no response. We knocked again and heard a faint response. "Hey, good morning in there. You alive?" "Yeah, give me a second." He opened the door in his underwear, obviously embarrassed. The room was redolent with the smell of sex, as Michael and I mumbled our apologies. He rummaged around the room for a minute, found a pair of jeans, and struggled to put them on. We noticed he tried to kick a sex toy under the bed as he struggled with his pants. He finally decided he was in no condition to join our day out. He apologized once more as Michael and I fled down the hall to the elevator, giggling like grade schoolers.

We went down to breakfast and began a leisurely walk down the river and past Osaka Castle. It was a beautiful spring day, and the cherry blossoms were in bloom. We reached the Panasonic building before it opened. We watched through the lobby as all Panasonic employees did their morning ritual of exercises. At this time, Panasonic and other Japanese companies were at the cutting edge of technologies and advancements. This center enabled us to test out hands-on devices, phones, videos, and headsets. We came to an area and were invited to be in a video which offered several video choices. This had to be the beginning of the AI craze, which we are now very much a part of. I agreed to have this video done, and looking back, it was one of the silliest things I've ever done, but we were having fun that day, so I acquiesced. I was to pose and look suggestively over the mountains and valleys, passing the pyramids, the Eiffel Tower, the Statue of Liberty, and the Great Wall as I took a magic carpet ride. The ending tagline in broken English was, "Time to go back to Osaka now." We walked away laughing, and I'm sure I have never lived that cringe-worthy video down.

As for Michael, our flights together then, and our friendship, have remained a constant in my life. He is someone I have always felt lucky to know and to call a friend.

Chapter 13

Palm Springs

My flying out of LA became more predictable when I held a schedule and no longer had to sit on reserve for call-outs. I could visit my family back in Texas and had time to take my mom on trips when I had blocks of days off. She loved to go, even though she was a nervous flyer, but the trips took her out of her comfort zone. My father had been old school and had never flown on an aircraft in his lifetime.

I reconnected with my training classmate from Gulf Air, who was now flying for another major airline. She came for a visit on one of her blocks of days off. We did the town in LA style, and it was fun to show her my town, which had become a second home to me. We went to Venice Beach and shopped in Beverly Hills. We made plans to take her to the Beverly Hills Hotel and the Polo Lounge for lunch. We drove into the hotel, left the car with the valet parking attendant, and enjoyed lunch in this opulent hotel. As we were leaving and waiting under the porte-cochère for the car, the irony of the situation set in. One after another, the cars were brought up, and the valet announced, "The Bentley, the Rolls Royce, the Mercedes," and then came our car, as he loudly announced, "Toyota." We looked around as if to say, "I wonder whose car that is," trying to look as if we belonged, and then hastily jumped into our Toyota and took off. We had a good laugh at the irony of the situation, but I had grown used to it after working in that town for so many years. I had even taken the 91 S bus to work during my Neiman Marcus days.

This was the time we began to reconsider living in LA. We started spending more and more time in Palm Springs, which was a short drive from LA. I had been coming to Palm Springs since the seventies. I loved the desert. Palm Springs wasn't just a resort for the rich and famous; the desert lifestyle was relaxed and peaceful. The town of Bob Hope, Frank Sinatra, and Dinah Shore was where Hollywood had always come to hide away. So much has gone on behind these walled communities since the days of Rudolph Valentino, Lucy and Ricky, Liberace, and Rock Hudson.

We made the decision hastily one weekend. It was a requirement that flight crews had to live within a hundred miles of their flight base to ensure they could make their check-ins and flights on time. It was time for him to leave his studio job, and Palm Springs was within the legal limit (barely) drive-wise to LA airport.

We found a house and made the move. It took some time for me to adjust to the commute, and very often the drive into LA with traffic would cut into check-in time. This was also when I was still on reserve call-out, so later I decided to take a commuter pad back in LA and be home in Palm Springs on my days off.

I struggled to make things work. I found a small studio apartment in Silver Lake in an old house that cascaded down the hill. It was something I could afford, and it was built below the main house with a wall of windows that overlooked the city and the terrace below.

I drove in from Palm Springs the morning my on-call days began. The guys upstairs in the main house, who owned the apartment, were gone on extended trips. I was alone in the house. As with all on-call days, there was the interminable wait. You were at the command of crew scheduling, which often made me feel trapped. I relaxed on the lower deck as it was a sunny and mild January day in LA. I turned in for the night, with my cell by my side, waiting for a call.

Something jarred me from a deep sleep and jostled me to the floor. For God's sake, I thought, what the hell? I could hear the ceiling beams creak and the sounds of crashing and glass breaking all around me. I looked out the window overlooking the city, and I could see transformers across the city spewing sparks. I gathered my senses and realized this was an earthquake, a big one. Having lived so long in Los Angeles, I was used to earthquakes and tremors, but nothing of this magnitude. The advice is to stand under a door frame or in a closet, but in that moment, half asleep and with my adrenaline pumping out of fear, I just wanted to get outside. I was afraid the house would come tumbling down the hill on top of me. I grabbed for the deck door, but something had jammed it in place. I turned around, and as if by some unknown hand of fate, the window next to the door flew open. I crawled out the window and stumbled down the steps in the dark, trying to get my bearings, cursing under my breath. I scrambled to my feet, and I could hear someone on the next-door deck screaming, "Neighbor, neighbor, anyone down there?" I looked up, and in the moonlight, I could see my neighbor on his balcony, stark naked, calling down to me. "I tripped my burglar bars, and I've locked myself out." I paused for a moment before answering. The tremors had subsided, but the aftershocks continued. It was 4:30 in the morning. "I can't help you with the burglar bars, but let me try to get back inside, and I'll get you some underwear or clothes." I climbed back through the window. All the power was out, so I grabbed my flashlight from my flight bag and rummaged for some clothes. I put on jeans and a sweatshirt, grabbed my cell phone, and tossed my neighbor some clothes. He was grateful, said he had found his hide-a-key, and could get back in.

I headed up the side of the house to the highest ground, which was the street above. Several people were in the street, hastily dressed or in nightclothes. We all looked dazed and confused. As the sun gradually started to rise, the full impact of the damage began to seep in. It was a mess. Some houses sat at an angle to their foundations, windows were shattered, and potted plants were scattered. We all stood in the morning chill, but what was there to say? I heard my cell phone chime. When I answered, I heard some clicking on the line. "Is this David Edmondson?" "Yes, speaking." "This is Greg in crew scheduling. I have a trip for you this morning." He gave me the flight number and departure time to Tokyo Narita. "You do realize, Greg, there has been a fatal earthquake here in LA?" was my response. "The flight is scheduled on time," he replied. "I'll do the best I can," was all I could say. As I hung up, I headed back down the hill to my apartment, but the door still wouldn't open. I crawled back through the window, and the dim rising sunlight told the story. The door wouldn't open because a framed picture had fallen off the wall, broken, and jammed the door.

My phone rang again. It was the owners of the house calling from San Francisco. They had heard the news and were concerned about their house. They didn't know if I would be there, but they asked if I would go upstairs and check for damage. I agreed and promised to call them back. I had less than an hour to make my two-to-eight-hour call and less than three hours to make it to the aircraft. I had no idea what to expect on the way to the airport. As promised, I went upstairs to survey the damage. The house was furnished with expensive antiques and musical equipment, as one of the owners had been a musician. The carnage and mess were worse than I had expected. Stereo speakers had crashed through glass-top tables. Shelves of books were scattered, pictures were broken, and items were off the walls. I called them back and relayed the unwelcome news. They said they would cut their trip short and return home.

This was the now-notorious Northridge earthquake, which struck on Jan. 17, 1994. The aftershocks continued, but without electrical power. Thankfully, there was still running water. I took the fastest shower in history, jumped into my uniform, grabbed my crew bags, and headed for the 405 freeway. While the traffic was light compared to regular traffic patterns, the worst scenario was a total bridge collapse on the 405 freeway, directly on my route to the airport. Through backed-up lanes, I maneuvered past the collapse but had to locate another entrance to the freeway. I didn't know where I was going. Sirens were going off around me, and emergency vehicles were everywhere as I tried to snake my way onto the freeway. I actually managed to make it onto the freeway, but every traffic light was a four-way stop. I thought, I'll never make this flight. My cell phone rang as I tried to maneuver onto the freeway on-ramp. I answered, and all I got was, "This is crew scheduling, telling you that you've been cleared to proceed directly to the aircraft." Fine, but I still had a way to go to even reach the airport. I guess crew scheduling had finally gotten the message that there had been a serious earthquake. I was sure I wouldn't be the only crew member not making the flight.

Huffing and puffing, I walked onto the aircraft as the boarding door was being closed. The crew was genuinely happy to see me. I expect some of the scheduled FAs on the trip were unable to make it or just didn't try. Truth be told, I was relieved that I didn't want to sleep in LA another night. I shook my head, thinking, *What else will I do for this job?*

The Flight Attendant position has always required teamwork. Without organizational teamwork, a flight would never happen. There may be animosity between crew members or petty resentments, but there is always the need to support and inspire. After all, we were all in this together.

I was working a Sydney trip with a very senior crew, most of whom knew one another and were close in seniority. Most were former Minneapolis FAs who had flown back in the Northwest Orient days. I, of course, was working in the aft jump seat. Meal service was completed, and the movie started. We began to inventory the Duty-Free Carts in preparation for sales. Another junior crew member had agreed to assist on my cart in the left aisle. The two senior ladies were working the cart in the right aisle. We waited and waited for the other side to complete their inventory and finally decided to go ahead and start, tired of the delay. We couldn't start breaks until duty-free was done, so the delay was becoming an issue. We finished our sales down our side of the aircraft and parked the cart in the aft galley. I could see the cart in the right aisle hadn't moved. I noticed two of the seniors hovering around the jump seat. "Something's going on," I told my assist. I crossed over to the right aisle jump seat and saw a Flight Attendant with her head slumped on the cart while sitting in the jump seat. "Do we need to swing our cart around and do this aisle as well?" I asked. The two Flight Attendants standing ignored me at first, while one was shaking the seated Flight Attendant and calling her name. As they shook her, she appeared semi-conscious, slurring her words and drooling. "Should I call the lead?" I asked. "The lead already knows. You two take your cart and go down this aisle. The lead is making out the break sheets, and we'll be going on first break," she barked at me. I didn't need to ask any more questions. Clearly, the FA was under the influence of alcohol. Her friends may have been aware of her problem, but they were trying to shield her from passenger view and protect her. A Flight Attendant with that much seniority had so much to lose. Drinking, sleeping, or stealing were non-negotiable infractions that the union could not protect. These women got her to the crew bunks without further incident. She remained there for the rest of the flight, marked as sick (unofficially). We all hoped she wouldn't be drug or alcohol tested on landing, which was often done at random. Hopefully, with her friends' support, she got help or took leave—anything to protect her many years of service. Sometimes, you just gotta have friends.

Chapter 14

Dutch Treats

My friend Clare and I didn't get to work many flights together out of the LA base, but we were classmates and faced the same issues with holding schedules or reserve call-outs. She was from the Midwest and began to think about a base change. Minneapolis was not an option, but Detroit was. We talked things over, and I felt a base change would be good for me as well. Northwest started a new non-stop service out of Palm Springs to Minneapolis. This would mean a double commute for me, but the payoff would be better trips and better seniority. Flying was more diverse out of Detroit; we had the option of flying to Asia, Europe, or on domestic trips, depending on what our seniority could hold.

I began flying the Amsterdam trips regularly, sometimes on different aircraft types as the company brought on newer planes. This became a lifelong love affair for me with the Dutch people and Holland. How could it not? We were housed in the most luxurious hotels in Amsterdam, right in the heart of the city on Dam Square. My first Amsterdam layover was at the Grand Krasnapolsky Hotel, just across Dam Square from the Royal Palace. Behind the hotel was Amsterdam's infamous red-light district. I had been to most European cities as a tourist, but as a working crew member, I came to know my favorite places—sandwich and pastry shops, bars, clubs, and restaurants. The skies were often cloudy and grey, the weather cold and rainy, but there were always bright, fresh flowers, the smell of water, and the feel of history. After the long night flights, we were treated to wonderful Dutch coffee and sank into luxurious down comforters. I felt very much at home on these trips.

One memorable trip, we arrived in Amsterdam on New Year's Eve morning. The hotel gods smiled on me this morning, as well as the front desk crew. I was assigned a large room on the second floor with an expansive glass window that looked out onto Dam Square. The Dutch are big on holidays, and they may appear reserved by nature, but on Christmas (more on this later), New Year's, and Queen's Day, the town would cut loose. Before bed, I would stop at my favorite pastry shop right on the square for coffee and Hogen-Bollen, a Dutch type of donut, the best ever. I would walk around the square, nap for a couple of hours, and find a pub for some afternoon beers. I would stroll past the girls in their windows in the red-light district as they gestured to me. Hey, everyone has to make a living, and they made theirs in typical Dutch fashion: clean, efficient, and legal.

This was New Year's Eve, after all, and I was told that the Dutch had a unique way of celebrating. I arrived back in my room early in the evening. Dark was setting in. It was a bitter, wintry night, and a light snow was falling. My room was warm and cozy. I ordered room service and sat by the window. People waved to me, and I could see they were revving up for the stroke of midnight. So many happy people, most drinking and shouting, blowing horns, and ringing cowbells. Intermingled with all this chaos, firecrackers were going off. I noticed they were throwing firecrackers at people's feet as they walked by. Some got understandably angry, while others just laughed and walked faster to get away. This is when I saw what appeared to be a streaker, obviously drunk and feeling no pain. He had his shirt off and his pants down around his ankles, which restricted his movement. He couldn't exactly streak as he hobbled from side to side. Shrunken by the cold and restricted by his pants, he took a fall. He lay there for a bit, and two guys helped him up. They pulled his pants up for him, and he staggered off into the chilly night. It was another New Year as the clock struck midnight.

It was always fun to bid for trips over Christmas. During my flying career, I would always bid to work over Christmas for several reasons. I could hold better trips, usually the loads were light, and many Flight Attendants who had children or families wanted to be home to celebrate. Clare and I would often bid Christmas trips together. It was much better to be in a strange city with a friend than by oneself. Sometimes, our best-laid plans would go awry, depending on the trip and the location.

Our first Christmas trip together was domestic, to Washington, D.C. We arrived early that day with a light load from Detroit. We looked forward to a nice restaurant for Christmas dinner. Our hotel was in an area known as Crystal City, which had several luxury hotels and an upscale shopping mall. We checked in and met back in the lobby. Our first thought was to check out the hotel restaurant—surely, they would have some sort of Christmas buffet. Wrong. The hotel restaurant was closed. We asked the front desk for recommendations, and they advised us that most restaurants were closed for the day. We tried restaurants in the mall—everything was closed. We ended up with bags of junk food, and the hotel provided chocolate cookies, which turned out to be one of several dismal Christmas layovers for us.

For our first Amsterdam Christmas trip, we were sure we would have a wonderful, peaceful day in such a beautiful city. Amsterdam at Christmas was magical in many ways. Dutch pastries at Renee's, watching the mechanical elves slide down the wires from the grand ceiling at de Bijenkorf department store on Dam Square. Always fresh flowers, the scent of coffee or marijuana wafting into the street.

We met up to go for Christmas dinner at one of the upscale restaurants on or near Dam Square. We got recommendations from the front desk with directions, but they warned us the restaurant might not be open because of Christmas. We found our way down the narrow streets to the address, but the restaurant was indeed closed. Now cold and hungry, we decided to walk until we found something open. Even the sandwich shops were closed. We decided to look for hotels that might have an open restaurant. Feeling desperate, we continued walking by the flower market and came to a small hotel. It had a small restaurant that appeared to be open. We walked in, feeling the warmth of the lobby. We weren't dressed up, but we had proper attire for a restaurant on a cold and rainy day. We approached the maître d', who eyed us carefully and curtly asked a question in Dutch before reluctantly switching to English, asking if we had a reservation. We looked around and saw an older crowd, mostly Dutch and all beautifully dressed. We did not have a reservation, so he seemed very put out. He clucked his tongue and looked around the restaurant. I felt like everyone was staring at us. We both felt exposed and out of place. Every table was full. We were prepared to leave when we saw a waiter drag a square table across the floor and throw a white tablecloth over it. He placed two chairs at the table as the maître d' motioned for us to follow him. He seated us and handed us menus, which were all in Dutch. Knowing that most Dutch spoke at least three languages, we waited for the waiter. And waited. And waited. Others finished their food and wine and began to leave, and still, we waited. I looked at Clare, and she shrugged her shoulders. "Is this something out of *The Twilight Zone*?" she asked. "Maybe," I replied. I raised my hand to try and get the waiter's attention, only to feel like we were being ignored. Finally, he came to our table. We managed to order wine for Clare and a beer for me. We tried to make sense of the menu as the waiter pointed to various items. Finally, we gave up, pointed to some selections, and hoped for the best. We had finished our wine and beer before the food arrived. I have never been a picky eater and am willing to try most things, but Clare is a very picky eater with a particular disdain for tomatoes. When the waiter finally brought our food, we received plates of unknown origins—concoctions of grey-looking meat, pâté, and something that looked like cheese. There was also a bowl of salad greens with lots of tomatoes and cucumber. The Dutch are big on cucumbers. When I say big, I mean the Dutch are to cucumbers what Koreans are to garlic—it's in everything. We looked at one another, then at the food. "I can't do it," she said. "I can't eat any of this." We still had the feeling we were being scrutinized for whatever reason. The bread was the saving grace, but more than a hundred dollars later, we fled that restaurant dazed and confused. We arrived back at the hotel, still hungry, hoping room service might be open so we could order some food more agreeable to our taste. This was just another of Clare and David's dismal Christmas adventures.

Most of the Amsterdam flights out of Detroit were done on the DC-10 aircraft. It was my preferred plane to work on; however, the planes were aging, which meant more mechanical issues and delays. On one Detroit departure, when the flight path took us north near Canada, heading over the North Atlantic, there was a mechanical malfunction that triggered a warning light in the cockpit. We were forced to make an unscheduled landing in Gander, Newfoundland, the closest airport that could handle our aircraft's size. We had discontinued the first service due to the problem and had properly stowed the cabin for landing. After landing, the pilots gave us an update. They were hopeful it would be a quick fix but would know more once the mechanics assessed the situation. Passengers couldn't leave the aircraft, and it looked like it was going to be one of those dreaded rolling delays. We started doing water walks to keep the passengers hydrated, but the minutes ticked by and turned into hours. After two hours, we were updated that a part had to be flown in, and it would be a very lengthy delay. Understandably, the passengers were getting restless. The captain advised us to take out the beverage carts and give the passengers whatever they wanted. Still, the delay continued. It was into the fourth hour when we were given the go-ahead to resume the flight. It was a relief. If the flight had been canceled, there wouldn't have been enough accommodations for 300 passengers in the tiny town of Gander. I recall standing at the boarding door by the airstairs, taking in the brisk, clear Newfoundland and Labrador air, which was some of the purest I can remember. During the delay, the cabin had taken on a party atmosphere, I'm sure enhanced by alcohol, but it masked a seething resentment about the delay. We arrived in Amsterdam four hours late. Of course, as we said goodbye, many passengers voiced their anger about the delay. "I'll never fly this airline again," we heard repeatedly as they deplaned. But we all knew they'd never fly this airline again—until there was a fare sale or a cheaper seat, and they'd be happy to try us again.

I could regularly hold Amsterdam trips out of Detroit, and it was my favorite destination to work. I was awarded a trip working with a Flight Attendant I considered one of the most professional in the Northwest system. He commuted out of Dallas, was African American, and I believe he had flown with Braniff. He had an easy smile, a soothing manner, and passengers loved him. He could make a crying passenger feel like they'd won the lottery in a matter of minutes. I loved observing his manner of service, hoping some of it might rub off on me.

I was one of three Detroit Flight Attendants scheduled to work an irregular pattern. We would deadhead (a non-working flight unless the originating flight needed an additional FA). In this case, the most junior FA was asked to work, while the senior FA and I took passenger seats for the flight. We merged with the Boston crew for the Amsterdam portion, and my Detroit crew member, being the most senior, took the lead position. The flight was uneventful until we reached Dutch airspace. The captain notified the lead that Amsterdam Schiphol Airport was fogged in, and we were unable to land. Not only were the passengers disappointed, but most of the crew had plans for their layover in Amsterdam. We were diverted to Brussels, a short 40-minute flight away. The plane landed, and our lead was able to turn on his usual charm. Most passengers seemed to accept the unscheduled delay. They were given updated information and were advised the aircraft would be delayed until the fog cleared in Amsterdam for safe operations. Two hours ticked by. We did water and juice walks so the passengers would feel well served, but the aircraft was out of catering supplies, and the galleys were secured for the final landing. As time went on, the three of us who had left Detroit earlier were nearing the end of our contractual duty time. We were only legal to fly so many hours by contract, and after that time ran out, we could legally walk. However, we weren't at a regular Northwest station. The three of us huddled in the cockpit as the senior FA advised the captain of our situation. The captain advised us to remain with the aircraft even after timing out, which would put us in Amsterdam to continue our normal patterns. Our lead certainly knew our contractual rights, and he was prepared to uphold them. We huddled in the galley with only 20 minutes left before we timed out. The lead was clear about our rights. The most junior of us was still on probation, so it was a concern for her.

"You two do what's best for you," the lead advised wisely, "but when our time runs out, I'm leaving the aircraft." Of course, the junior FA was concerned about the passengers. "Will they still have the minimum crew if we walk?" she asked. "It doesn't matter—that's for Northwest to take care of. They can cancel the flight, deplane the passengers, or do whatever they need to do. We are out of duty time." He was adamant. "What about what the pilot said?" she asked. "Of course, he wants us to do what's best for him—remain with the aircraft so they don't have any disruption should the fog clear. He hasn't flown as many hours as we have, and if he had, I'm sure he would honor his contract and walk in a minute. Time's up, boys and girls. If you're coming with me, grab your bags and let's go." He was smiling as he said it. He stepped into the cockpit and asked the pilot to radio operations and send a tarmac cart to take us to the terminal. The three of us grabbed our bags, proceeded down the airstairs, and were dropped at Sabena Airlines operations. They were kind enough to contact Northwest operations, who arranged a hotel for us in Brussels.

We checked into a luxury hotel near the airport for the night with further instructions about our schedule to come later. We checked into our rooms and agreed to meet downstairs for dinner. The dinner was sublime, and we had a wonderful evening. We had no clue what happened to our Amsterdam flight or our passengers. The lead said he would pass along any instructions from the company as soon as he heard. Later that night, I received an update from the lead. We would be bussed at seven in the morning directly to Schiphol Airport to pick up our original pattern for the return flight. We had certainly enjoyed a wonderful night in Brussels.

Chapter 15

The Air Up There

The Seoul trip was a very senior trip. It was usually a holiday when I would bid for it. It wasn't my favorite trip to bid, but the senior ladies bid it so often because of the shopping in Itaewon, the famous shopping area in Seoul. It was also infamous for selling knock-off designer goods.

Most of the ladies on this trip knew one another and often bid the same trips. On the flight over, I was working upper deck service in the aisle, which I wasn't very familiar with. There were 26 seats in the upper deck, in the hump of the 747-400. It was usual business class service, but it was difficult for me because there were pull-down video screens from the ceiling, and being so tall, I would continually bump my head on the screen. Of course, I knew they were there, but when you're busy with a cart or running to the galley, you forget.

Also on this flight were the smells! Koreans love their kimchi and garlic, but the smell of garlic permeated the aircraft. I worked the coach galley during breaks, but on an aircraft, it is impossible to get away from the smells.

Cabin pressure does something to the gastrointestinal tract, which causes air to build up. With all the meals and snacks served and the recycled air, it makes for foul air quality in the cabin. Four hundred and four passengers with the same condition explains the never-ending lines at the lavatories. Certainly, the Flight Attendants were not immune. One of the senior ladies came into the galley and proclaimed she needed to decompress. "I guess it's time for a little crop dusting," she said, as she headed down the aisle to relieve herself. I guess she got away with it until a mid-cabin passenger stopped her. "I know what you're doing, so please stop." She just retreated down the opposite aisle and came back into the galley, proclaiming, "Well, I just got busted," as she finished the meal tray on which she was working.

Our arrival in Seoul was on an overcast late afternoon. It looked like dark was settling in as we climbed onto the crew bus. I heard the senior ladies chattering outside the bus. "Okay, hon, I'm going to go straight over to Itaewon. You don't mind checking my bags with the bellman, do you?" she asked her friend. I couldn't imagine what could possibly be so important at Itaewon after a twelve-hour flight that she would go shopping still in uniform. These ladies were driven!

It was a beautiful hotel downtown Seoul, with a view of the Seoul Tower. They had a wonderful spa and health club restaurant. I tucked into bed, exhausted, but I couldn't shake the smell of garlic. It was as if it had permeated my pores. The next morning, I made my way down to the breakfast buffet and ran into one of the guys I had flown with out of the LA base. He joined my table around the same time the Aeroflot crew came in. They were in their signature tomato-red uniforms with extremely high spike heels. The two male Flight Attendants wore the bright red jackets and ties. It was only a couple of years after the fall of the Hammer and Sickle, but this crew looked hungry. They loaded their plates and hastily returned to the buffet several more times.

I related the story about the senior lady who had gone directly to Itaewon still in uniform. "You must not be aware. These ladies come over here to shop and take things back home for resale. I mean, a lot of things. I guess customs has begun to crack down, so they're having to be more careful, especially with knock-off designer goods. Also, the company has been tipped off, so they're having to be extra careful. It's against policy to conduct business while working for Northwest."

I went to the health spa for a massage, but I couldn't escape the smell of garlic. I then decided to go to Itaewon to see for myself. They had dedicated buses from the hotel to the shopping area. This must be like shooting fish in a barrel, I thought. I saw some of the ladies on the crew who were in the throes of haggling over tables of designer goods. They failed to acknowledge my presence, so I was sure they were distracted by the deals they were making.

It was late afternoon, and I could smell all the food from the stalls and on the street. I looked up, and across the street, I saw a sign for Kentucky Fried Chicken. Clearly, I was a long way from Kentucky, but I had to go in. I placed an order, or at least pointed to a picture. I paid and was handed a box. I went up the stairs to the fast-food dining room and sat down at a Formica table. I opened the box, and what looked like pieces of a dried-up Cornish game hen rattled around in the box. My stomach churned. I couldn't even take a bite. I made my way back to the bus, ready for the flight home.

NWA Uniform

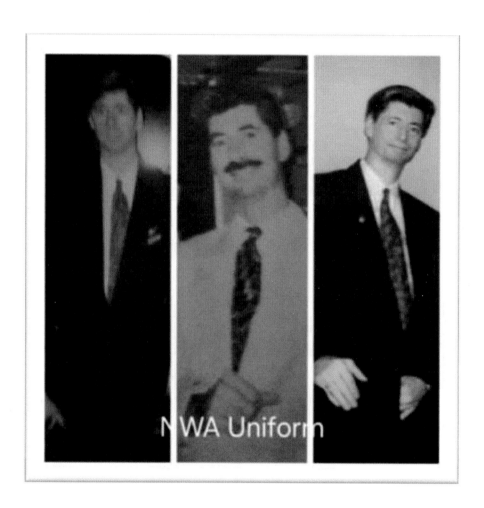

NWA Uniform

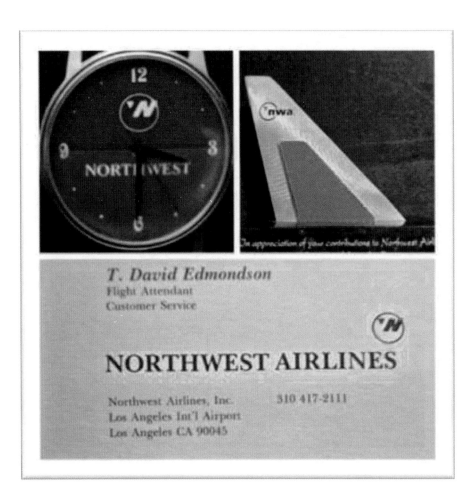

Christine and David

Michael, The Sky God

Clare, David, Christine
Sunnylands,
Palm Springs.

Amsterdam

Clare and David Christmas Beijing.

Trident Hotel, Laundry
Mumbai

**MAHATMA GANDHI'S ASSOCIATION
WITH MANI BHAVAN
1917-1934**

?avan is one of the few important places h
Gandhi's close association. It is situated
ad, Gamdevi, Mumbai-400 007.

took his first lessons in carding from a
?ass by Mani Bhavan every day in 1917.
g here. He y[...]
goat's milk here when his health was very
19.

Gandhi House, Mumbai

Memorial to Victims of Mumbai Attacks.

Chapter 16

Show No Fear...

As Flight Attendants, we are taught to show no fear. This doesn't mean we have no fear. We step aboard each and every flight with the task at hand in mind. Always in the back of our minds is the thought of what could happen or what might happen, but never that it *will* happen. I always felt it was an inbred faith that we manifest what we believe. There were many times I felt the need to call on this faith.

I was working a flight to Tokyo from Honolulu on the DC-10 aircraft. Our approach to Narita had been very turbulent. It was a plane full of mostly Japanese tourists. We had done multiple seatbelt checks to make sure everyone was strapped in. By coincidence, I was flying with a former Gulf Air Flight Attendant who had also come to Northwest. I didn't know him at Gulf Air, as he had flown out of a different base, but he was great to fly with, a quiet, shy guy, reserved by nature.

The galley carts were stowed, and we were both strapped into the aft jump seats at door four. The turbulence was terrible and had gone on for some time. It didn't seem to be getting any better. Usually, when the turbulence is bad, the pilot tries a different altitude to find smooth air. This wasn't happening. I assumed there was turbulence at all altitudes. I would look around the wall to check with him in his jump seat. We all handled such extreme turbulence in unusual ways. I looked at him, he looked at me, his eyes wide. He was shaking his head. Of course, there was nothing we could say. We had to be patient and wait for further information from the lead or the captain. The plane pitched and yawed, shook, and rocked. There were occasional yelps from the Japanese passengers when we hit a turbulent bounce. Finally, an all-call came directly from the captain with an update.

A typhoon had blown in from the South China Sea, and there was no way around the storm—we were caught in the middle. We were about twenty minutes out from Narita Airport, but the landing conditions were not good. We would need to be in a holding pattern. Diverting to another airport wasn't an option, as landing conditions were no better elsewhere. Also, we had a fuel issue and didn't have enough fuel to make a diversion. So, we waited. Repeated announcements to remain seated were made. The turbulence seemed to be getting more ferocious the longer we circled. Another all-call update: Apparently, a Northwest cargo plane had clipped a wing while attempting to land, and the airport was doing a runway check to make sure there was no debris on the runway. This didn't look good. I began to go over the emergency commands in my head in case we needed to evacuate the aircraft on landing. "Come this way, sit and slide. Come this way, leave everything, sit and slide." Still, we circled. After another interminable wait, the captain made the announcement that we would be landing at Narita Airport. He cautioned passengers to remain seated with seatbelts tight and low. The Japanese interpreter reinforced the announcements. I took another look at my colleague as he bent forward to look at me. "Okay over there?" I asked. "Yep," he said in a shaky voice. This wide-body aircraft rocked and pitched side to side, slammed downward in the storm. It felt as if the aircraft would turn over. Still, I ran the commands through my head. As we got closer to touchdown, the force of the turbulence caused a huge pile of magazines from the rack at door four to come flying down on my head. What? I knew I had to clear the aisle in case of an evacuation. I opened the lavatory door, began to kick the magazines inside, and slammed the door. At that very minute, the plane pitched to the right and touched down on the runway. This is why pilots are often known as heroes. I will never forget this pilot and crew. The passengers applauded; many cheered. As the plane taxied to the gate, the aircraft continued to be rocked by the winds. Only after the seatbelt sign was turned off could I see what a disaster the cabin was. Some overhead bins had opened, and some bags had been tossed into the aisle. A lavatory storage closet located at the bulkhead behind the last row of passenger seats had opened, and I could see the Japanese ladies brushing tampons and lavatory supplies out of their seats. Sometimes, in times like these, you gotta have faith.

I was working a Detroit to Amsterdam flight that seemed uneventful. We had finished the service, done the pickup, and we were in the galley with our meal trays, catching up on company gossip. Two of the seniors appeared to be getting into the years-long ongoing debate of red tail versus green tail. Southern Airways had merged with North Central Airlines in 1979. North Central Airlines then merged with Northwest Airlines in 1986. This must have been when the animosity started; I was never quite clear on what the problem was all about. This was before my time, but both groups felt like their seniority had been superseded in the merger. Anytime a green tail (North Central) flew with a red tail (Northwest), there was trouble. As the debate raged, I had my back to the right aisle with the galley curtain closed behind me so I could eat in privacy. Through the chatter, I felt something fall against me into the curtain, and I heard a loud snap as something fell. I flung the curtain back and saw the body of what appeared to be a very tall male, laid precariously on the floor face down below the Flight Attendant jump seat at door two. I bent down to turn him over, and blood spurted out of his chin area. He was unconscious but breathing. The rest of the crew in the galley sprang into action. The blood gushed from what looked like a flap of skin hanging from his chin. My first thought was to stop the bleeding, so I held the flap of skin to his chin tightly in hopes of stopping the blood flow. He slowly regained consciousness as the crew produced oxygen and the first aid kit. It was our good fortune that a doctor was on board. He said I had done the right thing in stopping the blood flow, but we would need to bandage his wound and get him into a seat. We got him upright in the FA jump seat to at least get him bandaged. He said that as far as he could remember, he just blacked out. He didn't remember anything after. For him to get such a cut on his chin, it looked as though he hit the metal surrounding of the FA jump seat, which caused the cut. The doctor was concerned about what a hit like that had done to his head and neck. We were over the mid-Atlantic, so it was decided it would be necessary to continue on to Amsterdam, with no real alternative for diversion. I cleaned myself up from the blood, and we continued with the flight. Certainly, there was no more talk of red tail versus green tail. The injured passenger thanked us all for our help as the paramedics met the flight in Amsterdam.

It was another Amsterdam trip when the unexpected once again took over. I was working the beverage cart, following the meal cart. We had well-stocked carts with all beverages and triangle plastic pots of coffee and tea for those who wanted something hot with their meal. We were almost to door three when my cart reached the bump in the carpet connector. As I tried to maneuver my cart over the carpet, the whole pot of coffee dumped into the lap of the passenger seated on the aisle. I was mortified. I pushed the cart to door three and ran back to the galley to grab anything absorbent to try to clean up the situation. My real concern was that he might be burned, so I asked if he wanted ice. This passenger was a very understanding man. He realized accidents happen, but I wanted to do anything I could to try to make things better. His shirt was soaked in coffee, though his pants weren't as bad. The Flight Attendant working the aft beverage cart picked up the slack and completed the service for me. There's only so much that can be done in a situation like this. I offered him one of my own shirts to wear, gave him cleaning vouchers, bottles of wine—anything I could do to help him recover. He thanked me before deplaning, knowing that accidents do happen.

I would work many domestic trips when my schedule couldn't hold international. I was awarded a five-day DC-9 trip with several Detroit turns. My third leg of the day was a Detroit to Raleigh-Durham leg, and a short layover in Raleigh. I didn't feel like being lead for a whole four-day multi-trip pattern, so I took the aft position in the dreaded tail cone. It was a light passenger load and an easy trip down; however, as we approached the airport, we appeared to be flying into a storm. We did the aisle check early and strapped into our jump seats. Oddly enough, we had gotten no arrival announcements from the cockpit. The lead had been flying less than a year. The visibility from the jump seat on this aircraft is poor in that you have to really lean forward to see out of the aft windows. We circled and circled, and still no updates from the captain. It was a two-person cockpit, and when the crew got on, the captain made no introduction to the crew (crew coordination is mandatory on any flight), and the two didn't appear to be speaking to one another. Difficult day or bad attitudes from the cockpit crew, I assumed. Still, I had a bad feeling. I was strapped into that back jump seat, with weather conditions, turbulence, and no communication from up front. We continued to circle. I called the lead to ask her what was going on. She said she had gotten no information from the cockpit and didn't want to call if they were dealing with weather-related problems. I had deferred lead to her, so there was nothing I could say, but we certainly had every right to be kept informed if there were problems concerning landing or safety. We continued to circle, and finally, I felt the plane lower altitude, and the landing gear went down. The turbulence was terrible, and I took it upon myself to get on the PA and remind everyone to remain seated with their seatbelts fastened. I craned my neck to check conditions. It looked grey and windy, but I didn't see rain. We touched down quickly, but when I expected the power back of the engines, I heard the engine thrust as the plane tried to gain power to take off again. This was bad. I felt like the engines couldn't gain enough power for another takeoff before we ran out of runway. I was thinking about the tail cone exit procedures and what I would need to do in an evacuation. Finally, the aircraft lifted off again to regain altitude. Still no communication from the cockpit. We appeared to be doing another go-around. Something was not right. Still, I refreshed the tail cone release procedures in my head. I was not only nervous but angry, feeling the cabin crew had been left with no communication whatsoever. This did not follow crew communication procedures, especially in an aircraft- and safety-related crisis. The passengers kept looking back at me as I tried to keep a calm demeanor. The plane made one last go-around and finally landed, rocked by the wind. Thankfully, we safely deplaned all passengers, and before I could get to the forward cabin, the cockpit crew had grabbed their bags, headed down the jetway, and were gone. I asked the lead if the captain had given her any kind of information as to what had happened. "Nothing," she said as she grabbed her crew bag. "I can tell you one thing—if we have the same crew leaving out of here in the morning, I'm not going. I will be suddenly sick or fall down in the jetway, but I'm not going anywhere with those guys again," was my response. I was livid. She agreed. I got the crew names off the manifest and considered calling the company over such a blatant breakdown of protocol, which was entirely safety-related. As it turned out, the next day's flights were rescheduled, and I never saw that crew again.

Chapter 17

Go Where You Can, When You Can

One would think that working on an aircraft would make you not want to be on one during days off. However, travel and your pass benefits are primary reasons for taking the job. Many of my Flight Attendant friends were always willing to take a trip to an interesting or exotic destination anytime we could work out our days off.

My best girls at Northwest, Clare and Christine, scheduled our days off together so we could take a trip to New Orleans. They had been there before, but I wanted to show them the town as I knew it. The three of us scheduled a room at a French Quarter hotel. We took the streetcar uptown, strolled through Jackson Square, hit all the restaurants, and covered ourselves with powdered sugar from Café Du Monde. Later, around sundown, we started our pub crawl on Bourbon Street. While Bourbon Street might be a huge cliché, if you drink enough, it's always fun. We hit all the bars: strip bars, gay bars, leather bars, and rock bars. We were having so much fun. We went into a bar that had an ear-splitting rock band. Everyone was dancing or, at the very least, slamming into one another. It came off as some sort of Cajun body slam, but we continued to maneuver through the crowd. A couple of guys ogled the girls and wanted to join the fun. From somewhere in the crowd, a rubber condom hat was placed on Christine's head, who proceeded to pass it to Clare. Someone tried to place the hat on my head, but hey, this is where I had to draw the line. Something about a six-foot-two male in a condom hat didn't appeal to me, so it was back to Christine, who had obviously bonded with a handsome sailor. Clare shouted in my direction that we had better get out of there while we still had a grip on Christine. We headed further down Bourbon, pondering having a Hurricane, but changed our minds and decided it was time to head back to the hotel. As we turned the corner, we realized the sailor was still stalking Christine. He kept calling her name. I could tell Clare was concerned about how to lose him before we got to our hotel. We agreed that Christine needed to let him down easily, and for him to quietly go away. She went back and talked to him, and we staggered back to our room. We got back to our room, happy but exhausted. We had early flights out in the morning. We were in bed, rehashing the night, and all of a sudden, we heard huge pounding on the door. Her sailor was screaming her name. Clare and I were livid that Christine had told him which hotel we were in and had even given him the room number. He kept banging on the door. Clare and Christine whispered in hopes he would think they weren't there. Finally, I said, "That's it." I went to the door and shouted, "Christine is not here, so get away from the door, or I'll call the police." That did the trick. Three friends in the Big Easy—one of our first trips together, but certainly not our last.

My next big trip was to South Africa, solo. The view from atop Table Mountain gave me a feeling as if I were on top of the world, and in some ways, I suppose I was. At the very tip of Africa, with the ocean and the city of Cape Town below, it gave me a feeling that not much bad could happen here. However, very much bad had happened in South Africa with its disturbing history of Apartheid. Nelson Mandela had just been elected the new president of the nation, which promised wonderful new beginnings for all the people of South Africa.

It was a twenty-eight-hour trip for me from Detroit to Amsterdam and on to Cape Town, on KLM, our SkyTeam partner. Pass riding is a wonderful perk—free or reduced-rate travel, with the caveat being, if there's an open seat. On departure day, the sky gods were with me. Schiphol Airport is the hub for KLM, and the airport is a sea of eggshell blue, the airline's colors. KLM and NWA at the time were the world's oldest continually operating passenger airlines. I spent most of the six-hour connection time in KLM's Crown Lounge after arriving from Detroit. It was a long, eleven-hour flight. KLM had the longest history of service to South Africa, as many of the early settlers were Dutch. The KLM aircraft had a tradition of dipping its wing over Table Mountain on approach for landing to give passengers a better view. This 747-400 did just that on approach.

I booked a beautiful hotel on the Strand, and upon check-in, I could see the Singapore Flight Attendants in their sarong kebayas in the lobby waiting for their pickup.

My room had a spectacular view of Cape Town, and I was ready to be out there in it. I walked the city in the afternoon and went to a recommended restaurant in the early evening. I was advised to always take a taxi after dark, and this I did. The restaurant had a lovely ocean view, with great food and friendly people.

The next morning, I was up early for a planned trip to Stellenbosch, the wine country outside Cape Town. I wasn't a wine drinker, but the lush valley and vineyards were well-known and beautiful. We passed Soweto, which sent a shiver through my thoughts, and I was back to the hotel. I went to the Company Gardens in the middle of town and to the church where Desmond Tutu officiated. I needed to exchange money, and the front desk directed me to a bank close to the hotel. It was bright daylight, and everything looked perfectly safe. I went around the corner and found the ATM location. It had several ATM machines inside. You entered by inserting your ATM card, and the doors closed behind you. I was the only one inside until a lady came in, but she was piggybacked by four ten-year-old boys. I looked over my shoulder, and when I saw them, I pulled my card out of the machine. One of the boys tried to grab my card while saying, "I help you." Another started pulling on my pants leg as a distraction. I've always been a cautious person, and I didn't feel threatened, but I did feel cornered. I started kicking at the boy who was pulling at my pants leg and saying, "I'll take care of this, leave me alone." Something I did or said must have spooked them. They all ran out the door, and the lady scurried out behind them, rushing in the opposite direction. I made a quick transaction, got my cash, and looked both ways down the street as I headed back to the hotel.

I wasn't so lucky on my return flight. Apparently, the flights to Amsterdam had either been full or had weight and balance issues due to cargo. I could be stuck there for days. I didn't have that option, as I had to get back to base; I was due to fly in two days. I had no choice but to buy a full-fare ticket on South African Airlines to Atlanta. This flight had an even longer flight time, with a fuel stop in North Africa. I would still need to get my connecting flight from Atlanta to Detroit, but at least I'd be back in the States. I did make it back in time to work my flights; however, the timing was cutting it close.

I have always been fascinated by the myth of Evita Peron. What made her so endeared to the Argentine people? Maybe it was her style or her speeches. Even after the treasury was looted and she squandered so much on her lifestyle and Balenciaga gowns, the peasants still loved her. I stood at her tomb in Recoleta Cemetery and watched as what appeared to be three destitute individuals lay flowers on her tomb. This woman has been dead since 1952, but the myth is alive even today.

Buenos Aires is a favorite place that I visit often. How can you not love a place with beautiful people, great food, and tango shows performed on the street? I would often visit La Boca, the colorful artist enclave in the city, during the day—never at night. A visit to Café Tortoni, famous from the Peron days, a hangout for film stars, diplomats, politicians, and a few dictators as well, is a must-see. It has a famous tango show. I often took Buquebus, the ferry from Buenos Aires to Colonia and Montevideo, Uruguay.

Leaving Palm Springs in the heat of summer was a relief and escape, arriving in the winter chill of Buenos Aires. The Argentine *asados* had the best food and grilled meats, and of course, the beef that Argentina is so famous for.

It was a chilly, moonlit night when I went to the *asado* close to my hotel. Bundled up from the chill, the waiter seated me at a table that gave me a wonderful street view. I could watch the pedestrian traffic and the street shows, always entertaining.

There were many children of the street, much like Bangkok and Mumbai—a fact of life for many poor countries. However, there was a difference in that these children appeared to be less aggressive, smiling and good-natured. Maybe it was my perception and not a fact, but some waved to me as they passed. When they would try to approach my table, the waiter would angrily wave them away. He would look at me and gesture not to encourage them. I guess they were perceived as a nuisance to the diners. My food was served, and I was about to order dessert. I spotted a young girl with tousled hair and sparkling brown eyes smiling in my direction. She was wearing a dress much too light for the street in the winter chill, and she looked undernourished. Something about this child tugged at my heartstrings, giving me a feeling I have never forgotten. I motioned her over and tried to communicate with gestures and a smile. When the waiter saw her approach, he came out of the restaurant to wave her away. I put my hand up to the waiter as if to say, "No." I pulled out a chair and gestured for her to sit. She sat there shyly for a moment and just looked at me as if puzzled. I gestured for the waiter and pointed to a picture of the cream tarts on the menu. "Dos, por favor," I said. The waiter looked confused. The little girl began to smile again, but still, she said nothing. The waiter brought two pastries piled high with whipped cream, set them on the table, and walked away. I placed one pastry in front of her. Her eyes sparkled. I handed her a fork and gestured for her to eat. She grabbed the pastry with her hand and took a bite. She had whipped cream all over her face. I laughed out loud as she happily took another bite. I could see she was getting restless, and she stood as if to leave. I motioned for her to come closer. I took the cashmere scarf I had around my neck and placed it over her head. "You take this, a gift from me to you." She didn't understand, but she *did* understand. She smiled as she felt the scarf and started to walk away. "Here, don't forget your pastry," I said. She grabbed the pastry and started to walk away. I saw her look back at me as she headed down the street into the night. My eyes burned with tears as I saw this little girl walk away. I have never been emotional about children because they always belonged to someone else. This little girl belonged to no one. What would her future be? This is a moment I shall never forget. The sight of that lonely little girl with whipped cream all over her face has remained burned into my psyche.

I decided it was time to make another trip to Bangkok. I asked a friend to join me and travel with a buddy pass on Northwest. We wanted to make a stop in Hong Kong and continue on to Bangkok. It would mean connecting in Narita for both destinations. Hong Kong is a most interesting destination. It is a place that reaches out and grabs you. First, the short and jarring landing over the rooftops at the airport. The high-rises built into the hills, some luxurious and others with laundry drying on the balconies. We were there when Hong Kong was still an independent state. There were still sampans in the harbor. The city bustled with commerce and history, and it felt like it was in a permanent rush. We took the ferry over to Macau, which had remained under Portuguese rule, but not for much longer. Macau looked run down and shabby, having long ago lost its luster of the great gambling parlors of the thirties and forties. Back in Hong Kong, we visited the giant Buddha and took the Peak Train straight up the mountain, which felt as if we were lying on our backs because the incline was so steep. We dined at the top of the mountain, which has to be one of the most spectacular views in all the world. On leaving Hong Kong, we would backtrack to Narita for our connection. The Bangkok flights were full, but we did get seats.

Our hotel was the NWA crew layover hotel, an ultra-modern teak and glass facility with several fine restaurants. We had high tea at the famous Oriental Hotel on the Klong. Later, we took a cruise up the river to the King's Summer Palace, which was nirvana in its beauty and location. We cruised further up the river to the ancient city of Ayutthaya, the former Thai capital from 1350 until it was razed by the Burmese in 1767. The acres of park and the ancient temples are near the Laotian border. The calm and beautiful setting is unforgettable. As we made our way back to the temple, an entourage of black official-looking vehicles pulled up in front of the temple. It looked strange only because no other cars or vehicles were allowed into the temple grounds. Several men in dark suits seemed to be following a very self-important-looking Thai gentleman. We inquired as to what was taking place and asked one of the guards who this man was. We were told he was the Thai Prime Minister.

Back in Bangkok, we shopped at the open markets, went to Patpong, and even tried the fried grasshoppers off a street cart. Big mistake! A huge chrome and glass shopping mall had replaced the old Intercontinental Hotel. Such a loss of history, luxury, and class. Progress sometimes does not wait for permission. Also gone was the dreaded bridge from my first visit, which had been replaced by the overhead monorail system and public transportation. On the last day of our stay, we were caught in torrential rains. It was the rainy season, after all.

We had an early flight on our day of departure. We were packed up and ready to go in the lobby by six a.m. It was still dark and overcast outside. The front desk promptly informed us that the city was flooded, and most flights were canceled. We walked to the front door, and the hotel entrance and surrounding areas, as far as we could see, were under water. A quick check with the airline confirmed that flights were canceled until further notice. Fortunately, we had days off, so we checked back into the room and went to the second-floor restaurant, which looked out over the area. We took a seat at a table by the window. I looked down at the ledge of the adjacent building, and it looked like a stream of something running along the ledge. Upon closer look, the movement was rats scurrying to get away from the waters.

Chapter 18

Life Gets in the Way

I reached a time in my life when I began to feel as if life in many ways was changing. Possibly I was the one that was changing. I felt like I was only going through the motions—the packing, the commuting, the constant being on the go. I felt like if I stopped, I would not get going again. I moved my mother to Palm Springs so she would be closer, but I was constantly commuting and unable to spend any time at home. Then we got the news that she was sick. I hoped she would get better, but we learned it was terminal. She had little time left. I continued to commute to Detroit, working my flights with that constant feeling of foreboding. I put in for a leave, which the company generously granted. Here was the only person who really supported my decision to fly. She had always been my cheerleader, my support, my rock. She passed away on a hot August day, and my life was forever changed. The airline flew her back to Texas for burial. This renewed my gratitude in a company and an industry that I was proud to be a part of.

It was going back to work that saved me during this challenging time. I still commuted to Detroit, flew to Amsterdam when I could hold them, and took domestic patterns to fill out my schedule. It was during this time I was flying a lot of Florida trips—Miami, Ft. Lauderdale, Tampa. These flights were always full and sometimes a challenge.

I had reconnected with my old friend from Gulf Air, who was now flying for United. We had not seen each other for some time, as she had been in a relationship and had been living and commuting to Athens. She recommended I meet her in Greece for a catch-up. I was flying the last day of a five-day pattern before my departure for Greece and would have a block of days off in Greece. I was doing a West Palm Beach turn and would be back in Detroit by nightfall. I was excited to be getting away for a few days.

The aircraft had cleared for landing. I was strapped into the aft jump seat with the other Flight Attendant at door two on the A320 aircraft. We had done the aisle check, and the cabin was secure until... I noticed that one of the galley carts was not latched down. I unstrapped and got up to secure the cart, and the second FA got up as well. I quickly latched down the cart, and at that exact moment, the sky fell! We hit an air pocket, and the aircraft dropped like a stone. It all happened so quickly; all I could think was that we were going down. Before the flight leveled off, my head hit the ceiling, and the second Flight Attendant's head came crashing into mine. She was knocked unconscious and was lying on the floor. I felt shaky like I might black out myself, but all I could think to do was try to get her into the jump seat so there would not be any further injury. I struggled to get her up, and she started to come around. Somehow, we both strapped back into the jump seat, both dazed and confused. I kept asking her if she was all right. I was not so sure that I was all right myself. Takeoffs and landings are considered the most critical times of flight, and we are trained that it is the worst time to call the cockpit unless it is a dire emergency. This was a dire emergency! We touched down on the runway, and I made an all-call. The captain said she would have the paramedics come on board as soon as we reached the gate. By this time, I had a terrible headache, a huge swelling on the top of my head, and a terribly stiff neck. The second Flight Attendant was leaning back on the jump seat with her eyes closed. She was blinking her eyes, so I knew she was conscious. I told her the paramedics were on the way. What the hell had happened?

The passengers remained seated as the paramedics brought a gurney on board. They informed both of us that we should be taken off for evaluation. In hindsight, this is one of the poorest decisions I have made in my lifetime. The passengers were deplaned, and they took the second Flight Attendant off the aircraft and gave her oxygen. They said they had a second gurney for me, but much to my regret, I declined. Yes, my vision was blurred, my head hurt, and my neck was stiff, but all I could think about was my trip to Greece. The captain came back and was so apologetic for what happened. Apparently, we hit an air pocket that caused the sudden drop in altitude. The paramedics had me sign a release that I had declined treatment, and we headed curbside for the shuttle to our hotel. It would be one leg back to Detroit in the morning, and then I would go into days off. Fortunately, the lead and the captain had done copious incident reports, which would be particularly important to me later.

With a very stiff neck and a headache, I boarded the Amsterdam flight to connect on KLM for the flight to Athens. With luck, I should be in

Athens by the next afternoon. I tried not to think about anything but getting to my hotel. However, I might not be the best company for my friend when I got there.

I checked into the Hilton and heard from my friend that she would not be coming into town until the morning, so it gave me the evening to rest up. My hotel was a bit of a distance from the Parthenon and the Plaka. My friend came to my hotel the next morning, and we had lunch. We planned to get together that evening, which gave me time to tour the Parthenon and the museums. The city was somewhat hilly, and I was not feeling up to doing a lot of walking, but the language barrier and accessing cabs were dubious. Also, the Greeks were notoriously anti-American, feeling we had sided with Türkiye during the ongoing war with Cyprus. My friend seemed to be going through a lot in her life, commuting from Greece, in a relationship, and flying her schedule with United. I did not want to go into the turbulence accident I had been in— no point—but the headaches continued. My last day in Athens coincided with a state visit by Bill Clinton. My luck! I was in the Plaka for lunch, and mass demonstrations broke out on the streets, taking place right on the route over the bridge to my hotel. I got into a parked taxi in the Plaka and showed the driver the address of my hotel. He started shouting at me, something about me being an American, and ordered me out of his cab. I got out and didn't have a clue where I was or how to get back to my hotel. I started walking toward the area I thought was toward my hotel. I reached a bridge that looked familiar. I could see crowds and angry mobs coming at me. I kept my head down and kept walking. I didn't dare speak English for fear I would be chased. I kept walking and walking. Much to my surprise, I could see the Hilton off in the distance. What a relief.

The following morning, as luck would have it, I got the last seat on the aircraft in Business Class, Athens to Amsterdam. It was a long trip home, and with a quick stop in Detroit, I was going home to Palm Springs. I would need to see a doctor about these headaches. Little did I know what awaited me.

Back home, everything seemed to happen so fast it was as if it was all a blur. I saw my primary doctor, who sent me immediately to a specialist who dealt with injuries of the neck and spine. I was diagnosed as having several crushed vertebrae, head, and neck trauma—in layperson's terms, a broken neck. I was reminded how lucky I was to be mobile, as one more bump to the neck and I could have been paralyzed for life. I would need immediate surgery. I didn't know at the time what I was facing; it would become clearer as time went on. Fortunately, I was connected to one of the top spine and bone trauma surgeons in the country at Eisenhower Hospital in Rancho Mirage. The trauma building was named after him. It was a long, tedious, and complicated surgery. So much of my future was in this doctor's hands. It took five hours and required cadaver bone to be placed into my neck to rebuild the cartilage. My flying career could well be over for good. I certainly did not want that. I had a career doing a job that I loved. Maybe the universe was trying to tell me something—something about poor decisions and priorities. Going to Greece was certainly a silly thing to do if it meant I might never walk again. Sometimes we do not know what we do not know.

It was to be a slow recovery—therapy, baby steps, insurance forms, workers' comp, and a neck brace to be worn in the hot Palm Springs summer. In dealing with the company, after about four months of therapy and recovery, the insurance company tried to coerce me into taking a ground position at the airport. At the airport? That would be L.A. airport, 110 miles away. No deal—either I was going back to the original position I was hired and trained for, or no job at all. Legally, I did have options. They continued to try this tactic. I clarified my position legally, and the insurance company and Northwest understood I would be coming back as a Flight Attendant or not at all. It was nine long months of inactivity and restrictions that tested my strength physically and emotionally, but I was going back to work.

I eased back into flying in Detroit and chose to focus on domestic and Canada trips to remain closer to home. I still did not have full mobility in my neck, so I needed to take things slow. When we were advised to take our seats, I was the first one strapped in. It would be that way for the rest of my flying career. It was the last gasp of summer, and I was enjoying my Canada flying—Toronto, Montreal, Saskatoon, Calgary, Edmonton, and Halifax. These trips had some wonderful long layovers at some of the grand hotels, which were built as stopovers for the elite passengers who traveled on the railroads around the turn of the century. These hotels were considered castles of the north, and they had been upgraded and modernized to reflect their former glory days. The flights were quick and easy to work, most on the DC-9 aircraft or later on the A320, and the hotels were superior.

Our crew checked into the castle-like Grand Hotel in Saskatoon—sheer luxury, and beautifully restored. Keys were passed out, and I made my way to a third-floor room on a landing near the elevator. The room had hardwood floors, which sometimes creaked when you walked, but the room had luxurious claw-footed bathtubs and separate showers. I placed my bag on the folding valet, and something caught my eye—it seemed like a flash went by my peripheral vision. I shook it off as maybe it was my head injury acting up. The room was very cold, and I felt the need to turn on the heat. Heat in the summertime? After all, I was living in the desert with sometimes 123-degree days. Didn't matter—this room was cold. This was Canada, after all. I made a quick change of clothes and made my way to the restaurant adjacent to the exquisite mahogany bar. The food was great but expensive. I finished quickly and returned to my room. Still cold. Looked as if the heat had been turned off for the summer. I found an extra blanket in the closet and tucked myself in. This turned into a miserable night. The floors creaked, and it felt as if the bed was disturbed at times. I kept feeling drafts of frigid air. Not cool air, but frigid air. I switched on the light a couple of times to check the time. It seemed like an endless night.

I was down in the lobby early. I could not wait to be out of that room. It was later that I happened upon an article about haunted hotels. Several of the hotels in the Canadian Pacific chain were mentioned, with the Saskatoon hotel being especially noted.

The Upper Peninsula of Michigan is a special place in the summer. Long layovers in Traverse City were popular patterns to bid. It is very much a summer town. Madonna is from this area, and it is an exceptionally beautiful small town right on the lake. The hotel we stayed in was a short walk to the main street of town, which had bars and restaurants and thrived in the summer. This was a wonderful place to try and recover from such a difficult and challenging year. I could only hope things would improve. I was working mostly low-stress trips for the rest of the summer and would consider going back to the Europe trips in the winter.

Halifax was another popular trip to bid in the summer, and my layovers there were special. I remember walking down to the water on the edge of town. I could see all the way to the bottom, as the water was so clear and the air was so pure. It was hard to get my thoughts around the fact that Halifax had experienced one of the greatest tragedies in Canadian history. On Dec. 6, 1917, two cargo ships laden with explosives caught fire and exploded in the Richmond area of the city. The city was experiencing one of its coldest winters in history. The explosions were of such a magnitude that they blew out most of the windows in the town, and many froze to death because of the harsh winter. 1,782 people died, and over 9,000 were injured. It was hard to put this into perspective in the now compared to the then. Who could imagine this happening in such a tranquil and beautiful place?

As summer moved into fall and then into winter, the seasonal changes in this part of the country were profound. Flight patterns changed, football season kicked in, and the flight loads to towns like Green Bay, Wisconsin, Lansing, and Grand Rapids changed as well. Our Detroit flights to Minot and Fargo in the winter could be delayed or canceled due to weather or ice and snowstorms. Sometimes, as we arrived at the airport in Rochester, Minnesota, we could see parked on the far side of the airport the Saudi Arabian royal aircraft, which was there to deliver the Saudi king to the Mayo Clinic for medical treatments. Icy airport takeoffs were often delayed—sometimes lengthy delays due to deicing of the aircraft. Sometimes in these extreme conditions, the plane could be deiced but not cleared for takeoff soon enough, and would have to be put back in the queue to be deiced again.

As I eased my way back into the European trips, my flying became slightly more diverse. I bid a London Gatwick trip that had a long layover in the beach town of Brighton, a short distance from London. Brighton is a unique town by English standards and has a storied history. Brighton in the Georgian years was considered a getaway town for the wealthy and elite Londoners.

Our crew checked into the historic Metropole Hotel, which was just across from the famous Brighton Pier. The Brighton Pier was the first original entertainment pier to ever be built. Constructed in 1881, it was always considered to be the finest. I visited the Royal Pavilion, which was considered a folly of King George IV, who was considered quite mad. He did lose the colonies, after all, but the Royal Pavilion is a must-see palace of idiosyncrasy. It was designed with an Indian exterior and a Chinese interior, but it is magnificent to see in a historical context.

I worked a trip to Frankfurt and celebrated Oktoberfest. I flew a Christmas trip to Rome. Christmas Day was spent at the Vatican, followed by an afternoon at the Colosseum, the Borghese Gardens, and the Fountain of Trevi. I continued flying to Amsterdam, as I tried to fly my trips back-to-back to give me a longer block of days off to be home in Palm Springs. Life was changing, and I was starting to feel a bit more optimistic about life. That seems to always be the case when the unexpected sneaks in.

Chapter 19

Skyfall

My alarm would ring sometimes at three in the morning in preparation for an early departure. I made my two-to-eight-hour call before I went to bed, hoping against hope I could get some sleep. I always slept badly the night before a departure, in fear I might not hear the alarm. I would stumble to the coffee pot, shower, and go through my morning routine. I would have my uniform hanging, and my shirt pressed, ready to go. I would double-check my crew bag for my required items: passport, flashlight, cockpit key, wristwatch, and wine opener. I would hustle out the door. If it had snowed the night before, I would need extra time for the car to deice. I would arrive at the airport parking lot, wait in the open air for the crew bus to the terminal, show my crew badge to security, and put my bags through the security scanner. I would hustle down to inflight for my sign-in and proceed to my gate.

Is this what the crews of Flight 11, Flight 175, Flight 93, and Flight 77 did on the morning of September 11, 2001? Did they follow their usual routine, never considering this would be their last day to do so? That this would be their last day to hug their kids, kiss their spouse, feed their cat, or pet their dog? Their last day to put that sticky note on the fridge reading, "Be home soon, love you," with a smiley face attached? Their last day.

The only mistake they made that day was to go to work. They must have checked in for their flights as usual, introduced themselves to their crew, boarded their passengers, and strapped into their jump seats. They must have done all these things as they had done a hundred times before, but this time, things would be different.

Flight Attendants are trained to consider all possibilities of what could happen, but we could never be trained enough for when it *does* happen. Flight Attendants must face each flight with some sort of collective amnesia about tragedies of the past. They are aware of the hijackings, bomb threats, terrorist alerts, mechanical malfunctions, and tragic crashes, but they cannot allow themselves to dwell on any of it. They are forced to store this in their collective psyches as events of the past that "won't happen to them." I can only guess that the flight crews of 9/11 boarded those planes never considering the possibilities to come.

In our collective American memories, most of us can remember those profound days in our history and where we were when they happened. Like myself, those old enough can remember where they were when Kennedy was shot, or Martin Luther King, or Robert Kennedy—and now, September 11, 2001.

I was having my morning coffee; it was early California time, with the morning news muted so I could concentrate on my September flying schedule. I was due to commute back to Detroit the following day. I looked toward the TV and could see smoke billowing from a building, which looked bizarre at first glance. As I turned up the volume, the magnitude of what I was seeing began to sink in. Watching more and more of the coverage and what was taking place in real-time, I couldn't begin to understand, much less accept, what I was seeing. Was this some sort of disaster movie, or was it actually happening? As the day unfolded and the horror continued, the tragedy became real—aircraft, buildings, smoke, crashes—almost too much to comprehend. As a nation, we had to comprehend, and in the days, weeks, months, and years that followed, these lives lost, the questions asked, and the horror of what we did know became too much to bear.

Like everyone else, I continued to watch the news and the narratives that followed. The unanswered questions about the motivations of the terrorists, the continuing death toll, and what was being done in the aftermath—actually, no one knew. What I did know, which was personal to me, was that airlines and flight crews were involved. Flights, crews, and airports across the country were shut down and grounded. Planes had been taken out of the sky immediately. Nothing would be taking off or landing for days, possibly weeks, and no one knew for how long. I continued to receive updates from the company, but updates were useless when nothing was known. How could we get directives when there were so many unknowns? If knowledge is power, then having no knowledge of what was going on had left us all powerless. Phone calls from crew members and friends were filled with speculation about who and what was to come next. News reports replayed the images of tragedy over and over, but there were no real answers. All I knew was that I wanted to get back in the air again. Many of my friends couldn't understand this. They thought some crews shouldn't go back anytime soon. But what if airlines and crews had reacted this way after TWA Flight 47, Pan Am Flight 73, or Lockerbie? What if, what if! The "what ifs" kept coming. We had to get past this while we searched for the causes and effects of such a tragedy.

One thing I knew for certain was that flying, aviation, and my small place in it would be forever changed. I got the call from crew scheduling that I could be scheduled for a flight pattern out of Detroit in two days. The scheduler made it clear it was not mandatory. It was complicated to get me to Detroit as so few planes were back in the sky. I was issued a pass on American out of LAX to Detroit, and I would be working a four-day domestic pattern after that. Security at LAX was understandably tight. My flight to Detroit, as I remember, had ten passengers plus crew. The crew made eye contact with me as I was flying in uniform, but it was clear there was no desire for discussion—just a desire to get on with it.

My first days back in the air had an understandable aura of tension. Tightened security at checkpoints, check-in, and thorough cockpit briefings covered all manners of "what ifs" in this new paradigm we found ourselves in. We flew mostly empty planes for the first three days, and the loads picked up on the fourth day. I was the most senior on this trip, so I took the lead position. These were tense, uncertain times for all of us. In many aspects, we would all continue to look over our shoulders, to remain aware, to not just consider what could happen, but to consider it very well *would* happen. Security measures would be updated continually, and they would continue to be in the years to come.

In the aftermath of 9/11, it took months and even years to return to some sort of normalcy in the country and in the skies. I returned to international flying and to Amsterdam trips, where I felt most comfortable. I had friends in Amsterdam who were always fun, always supportive. I reconnected with a friend whom I had met with his group of friends at the Krasnapolsky bar. He was a distant cousin of Queen Juliana and the House of Orange through his aristocratic mother. When I met him, he was suffering through a traumatic divorce from the woman he loved, and I was trying to recover from the grief of the loss of my mother. He was open, always generous, sharing his friends and his home. He owned a magnificent apartment on Herengracht, overlooking a beautiful canal just behind the Krasnapolsky. We would meet up with his friends, go to underground pubs and wonderful restaurants around Dam Square. Amsterdam, much like New Orleans, was always a party town. The difference was the vibe of the people. The Dutch are very practical and efficient people who come off as very reserved. However, to open them up is like a Pandora's Box of feelings, emotion, laughter, and fun. The drunken Brits and the tourists on Dam Square were always out for a fun time. It is so different to see the eyes of a city through a local, and I came to love Amsterdam, and I felt very at home there. I often considered living there, but never made that commitment. My commute from Palm Springs to Detroit was tough enough, but Amsterdam to Detroit? No!

Our layover hotel in Amsterdam had changed, and we were on the far north side of the city. To get into the city center, we were required to take a hotel-provided van or make the ten-minute walk down the canal to the ferry, which took us across the bay. The ferry landing was at the back entrance of the train station and also had an outlet for the wonderful Albert Heijn supermarket chain, which was a must-stop on the way back to the hotel.

I met up with my friends on the last night of the layover and needed to get back to my hotel for an early lobby pickup. I was a little later than usual. I dashed by the supermarket on the way out to take some things back to my room and headed for the ferry. The ferries were numbered, but I failed to check the ferry number for City North. I jumped on the ferry just as the ramp was being pulled and took a seat inside, away from the frigid cold. I was exhausted from a long day, and it felt good to just sit. The ferry ride usually took no more than fifteen minutes, but this ride seemed to be taking an unusually long time. I got up and looked around, and all I could see were the lights of the city and the train station fading in the distance. What? I had gotten on the wrong ferry. I had no clue if this ferry would make a return or where it was going. I saw a couple huddled outside by the rail. I asked them where this ferry was headed, mentioning that I thought I was on the City North ferry. No, they explained, I was on the ferry heading to an area further outside the city, an area with which I was unfamiliar. I was in a mild state of panic. They explained to me that they thought this would be the last return back to the city, but they were not sure. This couple could see my concern and confusion. "If this ferry is not making a return to City North, you can get off the ferry with us, and we will drive you back to your hotel," the lady said. I was dumbfounded that someone could make such an offer to a complete stranger, but these are the Dutch—kind and caring. The ferry did make its last return into the city, and as luck would have it, I caught the last ferry to City North just in time.

The early lobby pickups were my favorite at this hotel. I would go down early for coffee and the wonderful ham and brie sandwich on the hard French bread. There was always a smiling Naomi in the coffee bar early in the mornings. She was a special lady, and it was always a delight to see her. She was from Accra, Ghana, and always had a smile as big as her heart. I sometimes miss many things about those trips to Amsterdam, but I will never forget the smiling Naomi.

Chapter 20

The Queen's Necklace

India, magical, spiritual India. So much has been said about this country—so many myths, many distortions. There is so much conflict of thought about this country, especially by western standards: the poverty, the homelessness, the foul air, the environmental waste, the destitution, and the pollution. Much of this is true and real, but this is also a country soon to be the most populous in the world, with the world's largest democracy. It shares eight religions all under one flag, produces the most films worldwide, ranks seventh in size, and has given the world Gandhi and the Taj Mahal. The Indians are also physically beautiful people, having won three Miss Universe titles and six Miss World titles. India also has mind-numbing poverty, homelessness, and pollution. But for me, amid this dichotomy, one thing prevails: humanity.

I knew nothing about India when I began flying these trips. They were very senior trips at first, but eventually, I found them on my schedule. These were seven-day bid patterns: Detroit-Amsterdam layover, Amsterdam-Mumbai layover, Mumbai-Amsterdam layover, and Amsterdam-Detroit. We had a full crew of Flight Attendants, plus an Indian interpreter. We landed in Mumbai in the evenings with an average of eight hours and fifty minutes of flight time. These flights were far different from any others in our system. Much more cultural and religious awareness was required. There were several religions, languages, and special meals to accommodate. We had Hindu meals, which are primarily vegetarian, and others that limited certain types of animal protein. Muslim meals allowed meat, and Parsi meals also included meat. Then there was the water. Water is the most precious commodity in India. On a full aircraft, we were required to do water walks often during the flight. As you walked through, the passengers would collectively grab for water, but strangely, they only wanted about a quarter cup each time. It took me a few Mumbai flights to understand the Indian connection to water. I asked the interpreter why they didn't bring their own water, and it was explained that they complained the water bottles leaked. Indian mothers usually expected us to provide everything for their babies. We kept baby bottles on board, but these mothers often had strange requests. They wanted the bottles warmed and asked us to add sugar to the milk. Sugar for infants? Cows are considered sacred in India, revered, but most cows are underfed, which created bitter or sour milk. Most babies wouldn't drink this milk, so the mothers would add sugar to make it more palatable. Who knows what the rates of juvenile diabetes would be in the future, but that's a debate for another time. We would add sugar to the milk, hoping the babies would have a peaceful flight.

The ancient caste system still came into play on these flights. Upper-caste women would often fly with a servant (usually in business class) to handle their every need, and I do mean *every* need. Those who flew without their servants considered their Flight Attendants to be their personal servants. They expected us to adjust their seats, smooth their pillows and blankets, and escort them to the lavatory—not just to the lavatory, but *in* the lavatory. This often led to frank discussions between the passenger and the interpreter.

My first landing in Mumbai was unforgettable. The India flights were boarded with canisters of disinfectant, which the Flight Attendants were required to spray until empty throughout the cabin and lavatories. This was supposed to quell any airborne diseases. It was never considered, however, what these chemicals could do to the respiratory system when inhaled. Flight Attendants would hold towels over their faces (before we had masks) for protection, but there was no way to avoid this practice. There was certainly nowhere to run. We had to return the empty canisters to be verified as fully emptied.

I was strapped into my jump seat at door four, and looking out the porthole window, I could see the hazy ground lights of Mumbai airport. I was suddenly struck by an overpowering stench that caught in my throat and was so powerful it tested my gag reflex. The best way to describe this smell would be as a combination of rotting flesh and raw sewage. I thought all the lavatories on the plane had backed up at the same time. The senior Flight Attendant, who had flown these trips many times, casually informed me that this was the smell of Mumbai. "Welcome to India," she said with a smile.

We landed at the old Mumbai airport, which was another shock. At first glance, we entered vast arrival halls painted a sickly green, with dim, neon-yellow overhead lighting casting an unpleasant glow. I was near the back of the crew line as we waited to get through customs and immigration with our bags. After a ten-hour flight, breathing this foul air, and standing under this dim lighting, we all looked waxy and ashen. I hoped that, as crew members, we would pass through immigration quickly. Not so. Indian customs had some very strange practices. I wasn't prepared for such detailed questions along with our passport check. We were required to run our bags through security upon arrival in India, as well as on departure. There were still many laws in place that were holdovers from the British Raj, especially concerning alcohol. The flight crew always brought in extra beer and liquor for the parties and gatherings in the crew room of the hotel. Insignificant amounts could be overlooked, but if too much was brought in at one time, it could raise questions. Often, the interpreter was put on the spot to explain why so much alcohol was being brought into the country, which often put their position in question. This was one of those times.

We stood patiently in line for what seemed like an interminable delay. Our feet hurt, and our uniforms stuck to our bodies in the humidity and foul air. At last, my bags were put on the security belt, and we continued a long walk past currency exchanges and car rental booths to the crew bus, which waited down a distant sidewalk, away from the shouting crowds and chaos. Stepping outside was another assault to the senses. Fresh air would have been a relief, but there was no fresh air—only fetid humidity. Before we left the aircraft, which was never done in other countries, we filled trash bags with leftover snack sandwiches. Upon reaching the crew bus, we were mobbed by homeless and hungry children. We began passing out the sandwiches, but there still weren't enough. I boarded the bus and watched out the window as those who didn't get a sandwich walked away hungry and dejected. This was my first lesson about India—about those who get and those who do not.

As exhausted as I was, I couldn't close my eyes on the bus ride through the streets of Mumbai. At this time of night, the streets were alive with traffic—taxis, scooters, trucks, and pedestrians. I could see lumps on the sidewalks, which, upon closer inspection, were humans sometimes covered with newspapers or huddled in cardboard boxes. I couldn't look away.

The bus followed a curve that bordered the beach and the bay. This curve of the beach area was known as The Queen's Necklace. Opposite the beach were opulent high-rise hotels and apartments. The bus pulled into the soaring covered parking area of a magnificent high-rise hotel. The Trident Hotel hosted film stars and dignitaries from all over the world and had an international reputation for service and luxury. Elizabeth Taylor had stayed there, as had Bill Clinton and many others. Our bags were unloaded, and we entered the lobby, greeted by a welcoming staff. Our room keys were distributed, and we headed to our rooms. Most of our rooms were on the eighteenth floor. Several crew members planned to change clothes and meet in the crew lounge on the twenty-first floor. Where they found the energy was beyond me. Crews from most of the international carriers—Air France, British Airways, South African Airways, and KLM—all stayed at this hotel and partied in the crew lounge.

I couldn't wait to get out of my uniform. I opened the door to a stunning room with a sweeping view of the lights of Mumbai. At this point, I was too tired to care. I hung my uniform in the closet and had to take a shower. Even in this opulent hotel, we all had concerns about the tainted water. Seeing the city for myself only reinforced my suspicions. Some Flight Attendants took care to block any body cavity from the water. As I stepped out of the shower, the marble flooring was so slick I nearly slipped, but I caught myself. I had heard the story of one of our second officers who slipped coming out of the shower, hit his head on the counter, and bled out on the floor. The very thought of that happening again did not appeal to me. What cost of luxury, I thought. I turned down the bed and felt like I was in heaven, but when I laid my head on the pillow, I was hit again by that Mumbai smell—it even permeated the sheets. Gradually, I would become accustomed to this omnipresent smell, but it would take some time.

I woke early, even after such a short night. I had a quick coffee in the room and remembered the senior crew members advised me to set my shoes outside the door, and they would be polished and shined within the hour. This I did. I went down to the tea lounge on the mezzanine for coffee and something quick. I was astounded when the person who served my table approached and called me by my last name. How was this possible? He had no room number and nothing to identify me. This was just one of many inexplicable incidents I would experience during my time in India.

I needed to get local currency and was directed to a cash machine across the street. I arranged for a quick taxi mini-tour just to get my bearings and a feel for the city. The driver spoke limited English, but I understood enough. What I came to understand even more was the begging situation. Each time the taxi stopped, arms reached into the windows—pleading, begging. Mothers holding babies, young boys with their hands out, all pleading in sing-song voices. I tried to roll the windows up before we came to a stop, but the heat was as oppressive as the beggars. All I could think about were the little boys who walked away from the bus without sandwiches at the airport.

India brought out such a guilt in me—the guilt of "having" while others had so little. It would take some soul-searching and reevaluation of life before I would come to grips with this. I was warned never to give in to the temptation to give to the street beggars, as there would be no end to it. I was told most of the young street beggars were controlled by older pimps who took the money for themselves. But some things I had to learn for myself.

One smiling little boy approached me, and I couldn't resist. He was so persistent, even though I kept telling him no. He wouldn't go away. He spoke English, so I told him I wouldn't give him money, but he could come with me. He followed me to an open-air street market stall. I bought a carton of milk and some cookies and took him back out to the street. I handed him what I had bought and watched as he ran down the street, the items unopened. About a block down the crowded street, I saw a man grab the items from his hand. The man took the milk and cookies back into the store to return them for money. Now I understood how things worked in India. I would slowly learn more in the future.

Back at the hotel, I felt the need to just get on with it, stop overthinking, and enjoy the layover. That is a lesson about the job of a Flight Attendant—you can never be sure if you will ever return to a certain destination, so the feeling was to take it in while you can. I booked the works at the salon: a massage at the health club, with steam and sauna. I returned to my room in a state of nirvana I had never experienced before. I noticed my shoes had been returned to my room, brilliantly shined. It was late afternoon as I made my way down the multi-level shopping mall connected to the hotel. Luxury goods at bargain prices, and I could see the Flight Attendants swarming the place.

One magnificent stall after another featured jewelry, precious stones, Indian crafts, artifacts, carvings, silks, pashminas. It was all there and affordable. Of course, you were caught in the hustle of each shopkeeper begging you to enter and buy, telling you what you needed. "Oh, you are Northwest crew, I have deals for you, please come in." I found my way to a shopkeeper I liked very much, and we became friends over the years. I would buy things from him, some I didn't need or want, simply because he didn't push. He was respectable and still is.

We had a 9 p.m. lobby pickup for a midnight departure back to Amsterdam. Everyone looked relaxed and pampered, but it was time to go back to work. We boarded the bus, and one of our Flight Attendants was already seated. She had her hand over her face and looked as if she had been crying. I was seated behind her, and as the bid sheet was passed around, I heard the lead ask if she was okay. She was, but she had gotten some sort of Botox or injection fillers in her face and had an adverse reaction. When I caught a side glimpse of her profile, I could see why she was so upset—her lips and lower jaw looked like something out of *The Elephant Man*. Fortunately, she was able to bid the galley position, which had the least exposure to passengers, but it would be a tough trip for her.

21

Bollywood

We would often have Bollywood film stars on board. It could be Aishwarya Rai Bachchan, Hrithik Roshan, or the Khan brothers. Mumbai was, after all, the largest film producer in the world. One of our Interpreters was an Indian TV star as well. Indian television had its own version of the Brady Bunch, and our interpreter played the part of one of the Brady Boys. Passengers would often recognize him as we boarded the aircraft.

I continued my India trips whenever I could hold them. I made friends there, and with each trip found myself more drawn to the culture and the people. I wanted to know as much about their history and culture as possible. This was certainly a country that could not and did not hide its flaws but was forced to embrace them.

It had been another long and tiring trip from Amsterdam, and it was good to be back at the Trident. Each trip I wanted to discover something different. I was still addressed by name in the Tea Salon by my friendly, efficient server, and I would enjoy my spa and shopping time as well. I now knew the staff and shop owners by name, and we always knew what to expect from one another.

Leopold Café was a popular restaurant in the Colaba district of Mumbai. It was originally owned by a Parsi family with a history that dates back to its opening in 1871. This was a popular hangout for Flight Crews and westerners. I was interested in the unique Parsi religion and beliefs and wanted to know more about their practices. It was a religion believed to be fading in size because of its structure and makeup. One could not join the Parsi religion, convert, or become a part of the religion. One had to be born a Parsi. I was told that the sacred Parsi burial site was just outside of the city in the hills of Mumbai. I arranged for a Taxi and a guide to take me there.

We passed through sections of Mumbai, which gave me a greater knowledge of the scope and layout of the city and its position in the bay.

There were endless suburbs and neighborhoods. It was early morning, not so hot, and I could see the juice vendors already out along the beach. We reached the Hanging Gardens, also known as the Tower of Silence, and the Taxi came to a stop. I asked if we had entered through the large Iron gates, and the driver informed me that we could not go in. This was a disappointment however, he proceeded to tell me what actually took place here in a Parsi burial. Parsis do not believe in cremation or burial as they feel it pollutes the earth and land, which is sacred. The bodies are brought here to the Hanging Gardens and washed and wrapped in muslin. The body is then placed in the large concave circular structure called a dakhma at the top of the mountain. And left for vultures and scavengers to pick the body clean and leave only the bones. This was interesting and telling, so far removed from the little Baptist church and cemetery of my childhood.

This, for me, was the real benefit of flying, seeing the world through a different lens, exploring, learning, to expanding my mind, my thoughts, and hopefully, my heart.

Clare and I managed to bid on a Mumbai trip together. She was looking forward to the shopping, and I was looking forward to everything, especially flying with my friend. I was not quite sure what her thoughts would be about India, but she was always optimistic and open about any new destination.

Our trip over, made me smile to look across the aisle as we did a water walk to see her balancing a tray of cups in one hand and a pitcher of water in another as the passenger thought she would be handed a cup of water. "No, no, take the cup off the tray, and I will pour you some water. Again, take the cup off the tray, and I will pour you some water," I heard her say. She looked at me across the aisle and gave me her famous eye roll. We both had so many moments like these.

We planned to meet for breakfast in the lobby and had scheduled a city tour which would give us an extensive overview of the city. Before I left my room, I arranged to send out some laundry and a couple of pairs of Levi's jeans to be washed to have ready for my Amsterdam return. I had no idea the value of a pair of Levis in Mumbai, but I was soon to find out. I met Clare as planned, and we crammed ourselves into a tiny, un-airconditioned Taxi. Again, the beggars at every stop. We stopped by the Museum, the Magnificent Post Office, and the Train Station, which were all built during Victorian times by the English during the time of British rule. We were to see the famous or infamous Mumbai Laundy. We did not know quite what to expect, but we soon found out. The Mumbai Laundry was acres of concrete stalls where mostly men, but some women stood in knee deep alkaline water and beat laundry with stones in the blistering hot Sun. It was explained this area took in laundry from all over Mumbai and had an extraordinarily complex tagging system to insure the laundry was returned to its rightful owner. This was another jaw dropping sight, as Clare and I melted in the hot sun just watching. Our next stop was at Ghandi House in a pleasant suburban area of Mumbai. This house was three floors, and this is where he held many rallies and meetings in his peaceful drive for Indian Independence. His library was there as well. It was moving to see his wheel and his sandals next to his palette as he had left them. This Icon of peace and the image of his face and his wheel grace the Rupee, the Indian currency even today.

I returned to my room and found my laundry had been returned. I took my jeans out of the laundry bag and was shocked to see that I had returned the worn and torn jeans of a little person or a child. These jeans would not have fit over my big toe. I called the laundry, and they sent someone up straight away, but I had a nine PM lobby call, so hopefully, they could locate my jeans quickly. My jeans were never found. I felt I was paying karmic retribution to the laundry Gods for my visit to "The Laundry."

I was to find out later that Clare did not share my passion for India. She was more of a Paris and Rome kind of girl. I still loved to work my India trips, and as luck would have it, I found a New Delhi trip on my upcoming schedule. New Delhi was a new destination for Northwest, and as it turned out, it would be short-lived. I bid this trip on my schedule not really expecting to hold it, but it being a new destination, not everyone knew it would be a Detroit bid pattern.

As the trip turned out, it was a similar inflight service to Mumbai with a different type of Passenger. New Delhi, the capital of India, flew more government-related passengers, Diplomats, senators, anyone on government business, as well as families and touristss. Located further north, it was a much cooler climate with a more diverse history and a different economic base than Mumbai. This was a longer flight in air time, so it was a bit more complex. The Indira Ghandi airport was more efficient and much quicker to maneuver. We did not have the crowd of children mobbing the bus as in Mumbai. I guess it is the nation's capital, that would not be a good look for the city, but I am sure they must have been there.

It was a beautiful hotel, of course, but I was far more exhausted on working this flight, possibly because of flight time, but I just wanted sleep. I scarcely remember falling into bed, but the following morning, I felt rested and ready to see the city. I met one of the Flight Attendants having breakfast in the restaurant and we decided to take a tour of the city. We bundled up and walked down the Hill near the Magnificent Red Fort, which was exactly that, very red, built from the red clay. We decided to hire a Pedi-cab. The cabbie was an English speaker and such a thin young man it was difficult to think of him peddling the two of us for such a lengthy ride, but he was up to the task. We were inundated with the people of the street as well, but the cabbie seemed to have a way of keeping them at bay. We went past the gates of the Red Fort and made our way to the Spice Market. One could buy anything here. We took our time to walk through the market, and it was disturbing to see all kinds of animals: chickens, ducks, dogs, and even some animals I did not recognize locked in cages, some much too small for the size of the animal. All I could do was look away.

The cabbie directed us to follow a man in white muslin flowing robes down an alleyway. We did not realize that we were being taken to a Hindu cremation ceremony. It was explained that the Hindus must cremate the body within two days of death so the soul would be liberated from the body and the spirit allowed to move on. Neither of us had planned on encountering a funeral by any means. I could see the discomfort on her face as the flames leaped into the air and the body on the funeral pyre was turning to ashes. As it turned out, she and I seemed to be more of the focus of the crowd than the cremation. We quietly asked our cabbie to take us back to the hotel. We were in a somber mood on the way back to the hotel. How does one find joy in a tour having just experienced a cremation? I came to understand in one of the most populous countries in the world death and transition is as important as life and rebirth.

Back at the hotel, I began to feel unwell. I took a nap but was unable to stay out of the bathroom. I realized India was finally taking its toll. As we reached the aircraft and began the flight briefing, I could tell by the rumbling sounds of our collective GI tracks we were all suffering from amoebic dysentery, the curse of India, also known as Delhi Belly. I was ready to be home.

22

China Syndrome

Our China flying began with the Beijing trip out of Detroit. This was a new destination for Northwest, and it would be a very senior trip to bid. Clare and I decided to bid on another Christmas trip together, and we were awarded the hoped-for Beijing trip. This trip, being new to the system, had many operational and governmental restrictions and safety guidelines to follow. Our in-flight briefing was more detailed as we talked about the dos and don'ts of flying into the communist country. Directives like try not to involve the authorities if it can be avoided. Always be aware of your surroundings and monitor your behavior at all times. Be advised should you become involved in any type of compromising situation Northwest may not be able to step in on your behalf. As with all trips, we represent Northwest Airlines, and our conduct and behavior should reflect this. Apparently, there had been an incident on a past flight where a Flight Attendant had left her passport in a taxi, and the authorities had been notified. I guess the situation mushroomed into a near-international incident, hence the warnings about our layover.

It was a long and uneventful flight with a nice mix of crew. It was Christmas and it was exciting to be flying to a new destination. I remember this trip well. There was a sweet and caring flight attendant on this trip. She had gone to the effort of bringing small, individually wrapped gifts for every crew member on board. It was not about what the gift was, maybe a small box of chocolates or a pair of Christmas socks, and it was all about the effort she took, the time, the care, to bring a little Christmas cheer at a time when we would be away from home on this holiday. This reinforced for me the basic caring nature of those that I flew with, my colleagues, and the industry I was proud to be a part of.

We went through a tightly scrutinized passport control, and I noticed the captain and cockpit crews were more closely scrutinized as well. We arrived at the hotel in need of sleep. We met early the next morning for a full day of exploration. The Great Wall, the Forbidden City, and always shopping.

First up was a trek to the Great Wall, built centuries ago, a thousand miles long to keep out their enemies. It was a bit of a bus ride out of town to the countryside. It was freezing sleet and snow, as I recall. We had to take chair lifts to the top of the higher elevation. These were open chairs that seated two. Since I have always been paranoid of heights, these chairs did not look safe. Given no choice, I climbed in. It was a bitter cold with icy wind and light snow falling. This was nothing for the Minnesota crew, who was used to these conditions, but I shook from the cold. I remember walking down the wall and looking out over the frozen, barren landscape. The trees looked like twigs with their barren, frozen branches. I could not help but think how many thousands of eyes throughout the century had witnessed this same view. This wall to keep out their enemies had not changed over so many years, but I expect their enemies to have changed.

Back to the bus and some warmth, it was on to the forbidden city. We walked through the expansive square, another part of history. It was Christmas day back home, but I was not home. I looked at the red temple buildings with the curly cue roofs that had been home to Chinese Emperors and Royalty. Somehow, this made me a bit sad, a bit homesick, disconnected from all that I knew. It was good to have Clare on this trip. Always grounded, fun, and petulant when provoked, but solid and caring. We had lunch back at the hotel. Clare was a picky eater, and I expected in China she would have much to be picky about. We were excited to be going to the huge shopping markets and spend the afternoon. From silks to jewelry to carvings or leather goods, it was all here. Clare was a careful shopper, so she needed to spend time alone to sort it all out. We ended up buying things for each other, and when all was said and done, we realized we would have to haul all this back on the aircraft, through customers, and onto our commuter flights home. Clare has always been a giver, a giver of time, laughter, and gifts. When we got back to the hotel, she gifted me a crystal ball I had my eye on in the market but did not buy. It was and continues to be one of my most prized possessions. After so many awful Christmas trips that Clare and I had shared in the past, this one was special. Who could complain when you are surrounded by history, holidays, and friendship? We all looked forward to getting back to our American lives, our homes, and our families, but so did those passengers we were taking back home with us. It would be time for a New Year.

Back to base in Detroit, a New Year was coming. I would continue biding the Amsterdam, Mumbai, and occasional Tokyo trips. After the holidays, the flying and the trips were cut back as the loads dropped off until Spring. At this time, I knew enough of the crews that I flew with to be aware of those that I vibed with and those to avoid. We would often run into crew members who had either been difficult to fly with or were just downright nasty. I was to learn early on how to practice avoidance in certain situations. Sometimes, it was just personality differences or a crew member who was lazy or unmotivated, and someone else would always pick up the slack for them. Some earned a reputation when you saw them coming, avoid them, or stay away from them. These judgment calls came with the territory, and I am sure I may have had the same effect on some of my colleagues as well. Hey, we were literally thousands of diverse personalities thrown together for periods of time with a job to do. Job is the operative word here. I think all any one of us expected was for our fellow crew members to do their jobs.

I flew a Tokyo trip which was a full flight with a minimum crew. This would require each crew member to do their part. In the predeparture briefing we noticed on the bid sheet a Flight Attendant with a well-earned reputation of becoming missing in action on any given flight. No one said anything at the time, and par for the course, she was late to the briefing and the last one to arrive, blustering about having to meet with her manager. No surprise there. She was senior enough that she could bid on the position that required the least responsibility, but it was a service position, so she had to be out there when the carts rolled. When that time came, she was nowhere to be found, so she held up the service. She had the stomach flu, she said, and had been in the lavatory. Really? The good news was that the lead Flight Attendant was on to her, had flown with her before, and she was prepared for whatever she might pull. She was European, and when challenged she would appear to not understand some things when it came down to her conduct. She was dumb like a fox. There was nothing that could be done about her. She could be written up, but there was an unwritten rule that flight attendants do not write up another crew member unless it is a serious safety or procedural problem. She was late coming off a break, which delayed the second break from starting, and she was late again to start the second service. We made it through the flight, and those of us directly impacted by her quietly seethed. It would be a challenging return. Of course, at the hotel, she was first in line for her room key. She was the first one in the crew lounge drinking, laughing, and having a great layover, for which she was also known.

On the return flight, things took a turn. We did our briefing and bidding on the aircraft, and she immediately began to complain that she was not well. She did not know if she would be able to work on the way back. Generally sympathetic to crew illness, most crewmembers would give a wide birth to someone who is ill and unable to work the flight. However, this girl had a history of becoming suddenly sick on the return flights. Her thinking was she would be allowed to be in the crew bunks for the entire flight while someone else did her job, and not be accountable for a sick call. Flight Attendants are only allowed so many sick calls until we are called on to produce a doctor's note stating we were actually sick. Most likely, this girl was out of sick calls. The lead Flight Attendant nailed her in front of the entire crew. "If you are sick and unable to work this flight, you need to commit to a sick call, and I will document this on my paperwork. It's up to you." The lead stated. She thought about it for a moment. "I will try to work for the flight." Was her response. "No try," the lead fired back. "You will either work the flight, or won't you?" "Yes," she answered. She worked the flight, but only after much whining and complaining about the way she was being treated.

I was beginning to tell that my time at the Detroit base was ending. The commute had become more difficult. I seemed to have less and less time at home in Palm Springs, and I was beginning to feel I was missing out on a home life. My trips out of this base had changed my life in many ways. I would miss them, but I would always have the option to visit my favorite places on days off. This would only be a change, not an ending. With mixed emotions I put in my transfer back to the LA base, back to home.

23

No End to New Beginnings

I would need to readjust being back at the LA base. The drive again from Palm Springs was always a challenge, which meant earlier wake-ups and longer departure days, and I began to fly Honolulu trips, with a few domestic patterns and an occasional Tokyo or Osaka trip.

The Honolulu layovers were relaxing, and I began to fall into a pattern. Having been to Pearl Harbor and the USS Arizona Memorial it was beach time or lounging around the Hotels. There was High Tea at the Moana Surfrider or lunch on the Veranda at Neiman Marcus overlooking Ala Moana Bay. Sometimes, it was fun just to take the Wiki Wiki bus around or just enjoy paradise. It is ironic to think how things would have been if, in training, I had gotten my first bid award, which would have been the Honolulu base. Everything does happen for a reason, but here I was flying these trips often.

On January 17, 1995, a 7.3 magnitude earthquake struck Osaka, Kobe, Japan, killing six thousand people. At the risk of sounding like an earthquake chaser, it was only a few weeks after the earthquake that flights resumed that I returned. They were still experiencing aftershocks at the time, but I was scheduled for the seven-day Sydney-Osaka trip on my schedule. Little had changed in Sydney, and it was time to rest up and recoup after the long flight. We were all a bit concerned about the Osaka layover and heard that the layover hotel experienced severe damage. I guess there was no structure in Osaka that had not experienced some kind of damage. I certainly had been through many earthquakes, and I lived directly on an earthquake fault in Palm Springs. However, to be in this town that had just experienced such a tragedy, which was still experiencing aftershocks I was uneasy. This was a sixteen-story hotel, and the higher up the room, the more jolts were more severe. The hotel seemed to be undamaged, but outside in the city, the cleanup was slow going. The elevated train had collapsed in some areas, and some buildings were leveled. My room was on the eighth floor, and I made sure to check the stairs should there be time in an emergency to get out.

I took the fire stairs down to street level and going down, I noticed hastily papered-over walls with wallpaper. I also noticed holes where it looked as if someone had stuck their fingers in the cracks. It was not reassuring when I realized the hotel had papered over large cracks in the walls after the earthquake. There were a couple of minor aftershocks but nothing of any magnitude, and I was glad to be returning home where the ground shook as well, but hopefully nothing like this.

My next Tokyo had an unusual add pattern, which involved a Guam Layover. There were two US Flight Attendants added to the south fly Tokyo crew, and one of us was required to take the lead. Most seniors would grab that position because basically all that was required of them was to make the announcements, and the south fly crews did everything that involved service.

I had never been to Guam before but had heard much about it. A twelve-mile island retained after the war and a large US military presence. I had also heard the island was infested with harmless green snakes. It was said the situation was so bad that the snakes had been known to crawl into the belly of the cargo planes. True or not, the situation did not appeal to me. It was a beautiful hotel built high up on the island with beautiful sand beaches down below, surrounded by stunning rock formations. This island was a top tourist destination for the Japanese. I explored the hotel and walked the beach. I ran into some crew members who said they were walking down to a bar, which was a famous military hangout during the war. We walked quite a way down and came to a ramshackle bar that obviously had stood the test of time. Entering the place, which was dimly lit with red lights, put a glow on the walls, which were covered with tatami mats. Lamps with hula dancers and calendars from the fifties gave this place a twilight zone feel. Our First Officer related that he used to come to this place on stopovers during the Korean War. I had a beer and left them on it. Nostalgia for them is creepy for me. The next day it was back to Tokyo and then a flight back to LA.

It was a very senior crew on the flight back. I feel this is the flight. I feel I made some realizations about my future, about my flying. I looked across the cabin, and I saw one of the senior Flight Attendants who had her back against the jump seat. She looked so exhausted, so defeated. This is when I decided I did not want this to be me. On arrival, going through customs, changing out of my uniform in the airport lavatory, waiting for the crew bus to the parking lot, and dragging my bags to my car, it had been a twenty-hour day, crossing the international dateline, numerous times zones, and still, I had another two-hour drive to get home. I made it out onto Interstate 10, heading to Palm Springs, and I was fighting to keep my eyes open. I stopped for coffee, splashed water on my face, and started off again. Still, it was not safe for me to be driving. I made it to the Cabazon rest stop and pulled over. I do not remember when I woke up, but I was ready to be home. I knew I could not continue with this kind of commute or flying.

The Northwest-Delta merger negotiations had been announced and it was inevitable this merger was going to happen. The crews at both airlines felt it was an uncertain time and were left to see how this merger would play out. Merger of seniority, route systems, aircraft, and company policies and vision. There could possibly be an overage of Flight Attendants and could possibly require layoffs or buyouts. All this was still to be decided. I had to decide what would work best for me, but I did know the commute to LA would need to change.

I put my bid in for a base change to Seattle. Yes, it would be another flight commute, but it would be an easier commute, even having to connect through San Fransisco. I would have the option to fly Amsterdam once more, or Asia, Maui, or domestic if I chose. Seattle was a well-run base with nice people, and it was indeed an easier commute. I received my base transfer award and began to make the needed adjustments. In my first schedule, I was awarded domestic trips with several Maui trips to complete my month. The Maui trip was a sought-after trip in the system, and other Flight Attendants on other bases liked to trip trade with Seattle to work those trips. The first few months in Seattle I flew these trips, and they were not what I expected. The pattern was on the 757 aircraft, a long single-aisle aircraft, which was sometimes a challenge to work. It was a non-stop flight from Seattle to Maui, but on the return, the flight was a red eye, which made an intermediate stop in Hilo. This flight was challenging enough to work because of the time and the stop, but also, the passengers were all sunburned and cranky, knowing their vacations were over and they had to return to their normal or working lives. It was a beautiful Japanese style hotel, a bit in need of a refresh, but a beautiful room with a balcony and sweeping ocean view. It also had a Japanese-style buffet with a thirty-dollar breakfast. For me, the hotel or the ocean, other than Oprah's house, which had no interest to me, were the only things to occupy my time.

I was in my Maui hotel room when I saw a Breaking News flash come across the TV screen. It was reported a terrorist attack was taking place in multiple areas in the city of Mumbai, India. The terrorist simultaneously entered The Taj Mahal Hotel, The Oberoi Trident, Leopold Café, and the Rail terminus. It has been reported that gunfire is continuing. The Mumbai police are seeking assistance to handle the crisis. We will keep you updated as this crisis unfolds.

I sat stunned as I continued watching. What about my friends at the hotel? What about the Northwest crew? How could this be happening? I was glued to the news reports until it was time to work the return flight back to Seattle. I could hear updates on the TV monitors as I waited for my commuter flight back to Palm Springs. There were reports of multiple deaths in all locations. I made my commuter flights back to Palm Springs and continued to watch the news reports. The terrorists had simultaneously entered all locations with the objective of killing as many people as possible. They targeted these locations as they were known locations for Westerners. The attacks continued for two more days. Bombs went off in the Taj Mahal Hotel, and fires were set in this historic building. There could be no real updates on the carnage until police were able to take control of the buildings. The Indian army had been mobilized to help police in the attack. This continued for two more days until the terrorists were killed or overpowered. Hostages fled the hotels. In all, 175 were dead, including seven of the terrorists, and another 300 were injured. It was almost impossible to comprehend. Northwest and other flight crews managed to escape down the service stairwell and others out the exit of the shopping mall. The perpetrators of the Mumbai attacks were discovered to be members of the Lashker-e-Taiba Islamic sect from Pakistan.

I reached my friend who worked in the Trident health club and spa. He had finished his shift for the day and had gone home just hours before the attack. He informed me the front desk personnel that had been the first to be shot. I remembered them, knew them by name. Kind, smiling, always helpful. Senseless killing with no logic, motivated only by hate. It could have been worse for the flight crews. Some had tried unsuccessfully to reach the front desk to settle their bills. The flight crew pickup in the lobby was for nine PM. That is the exact time the terrorist entered the lobby. Had they been in the lobby on time, they would have been some of the first to be killed. The shooter kept the front desk operator alive to make her call the rooms. Suppose the guest answered the terrorist, which room to strike next. They began a sweep of the floors, room by room, killing as they went. This was the Trident, and even worse was happening at the Taj Mahal Hotel, killing firebombs and grenades. Leopold Café was an open-air restaurant, a favorite of mine on my Mumbai layovers. Ten people died here when the terrorist opened fire from the street and tossed in grenades. Many more were injured. The tragedy that took place here on November 26, 2008, left its scars on the Indian psyche. A true testament to the Indian people is that the historic Taj Majal Hotel, which was nearly destroyed, was reopened only two weeks after the tragedy, and the Trident was reopened soon after.

The tragedy of the Mumbai attacks stayed with me as I continued to fly. The Northwest/Delta merger was finalized on October 29, 2008, and the Northwest name was erased from the sky. It was bittersweet for the Northwest employees who, for years, had poured their blood, sweat, and tears into making the oldest airline in American history into the fourth-largest airline in the country. The airline may have lost its name, but it had regained a new and stronger name in Delta. Not everyone was happy, nor would they ever be, but this was considered one of the most equitable mergers in airline history. Work groups were merged, and it remains one of the top airlines in the world. I guess Minnesota Nice merged with southern hospitality, and the airline continues to thrive.

I was measured for my new Delta Uniform. All the uniform pieces arrived, and I was ready to make that transition, but I hesitated. Delta was one of the first airlines I had applied with, but at that time, I was too tall. Another irony in the situation was that with the merger, I was not "too tall" to fly for Delta after all. Northwest Airlines airline had made all my dreams come true. How could I think about leaving? Still, something was telling me it was time to let go. The last buyout was offered, and I knew it was time to put my flying years behind me. I finished my last day of flying out of Seattle. I stepped off my last working flight confident I was stepping into a different life. I could still fly anywhere in the system at any time. I would be back to Amsterdam, to Mumbai, to Sydney. I would need to adjust from what was to what is and not look back. I would always find my place in the sky.

24

Don't You Know Who I Am

When I worked in Beverly Hills years ago, I worked on or rode elevators with or saw in passing many celebrities from Zsa Zsa Gabor, Diana Ross, John Travolta, Paul Newman, Lucille Ball, and more. It was always special to have a celebrity on the aircraft. I always felt a need to give them excellent service while trying to be unobtrusive and protect their privacy. Of course, there were always those that you watched their movies or listened to their music and felt you connected to who they were and felt the need to let them know.

I was working the boarding door, door two on the 757 from Detroit to LA. I greeted her as she came on board. I directed her to her seat, which was not in First Class but was in a coach seat middle, two rows back from First Class on the aircraft's right. That was odd, I thought. Here is an Academy Award-winning actress seated in coach, but I continued with the boarding process until I heard the call bell go off. I asked her if I could help her. "You certainly can," she barked. "I should be seated in First Class, and I don't understand why I am stuck back here in this middle seat," I asked to see her ticket again. "This is the seat you were assigned. I am not sure where the confusion happened, but let me check with the lead and see what's going on." "Yes," she said, "I am not about to fly all the way to Los Angeles in this seat. Something needs to be done." I went to the lead who was doing predeparture drinks. I explained the situation, and she followed me to the passenger. I introduced the lead as the passenger began her diatribe about her seat. The lead: "I can understand your frustration, but unfortunately, the aircraft is full. I don't know if you purchased your ticket at the last minute or what happened to your booking, and I am so sorry. But we don't have another seat to move you to." The passenger: "You need to do something; don't you know who I am?" She continued in a fury. The lead: Of course, I know who you are, and again, I am so sorry I do not have a seat to move you to. We will do all we can to make you comfortable on the flight. She then retuned back to her first-class duties. The passenger slept for most of the way after being comped drinks during the flight. She deplaned in a huff, not saying a word as she walked down the jetway. I can only imagine how the company would address that complaint letter.

Every working Flight Attendant has most likely served many a celebrity guest on board the aircraft in their career. I was fortunate enough to serve celebrities like George Burns, Tony Bennett, Mary Wilson, the Supreme Supreme, Tony Shalhoub, and many more. I flew the last remaining Tuskegee Airmen to the Clinton Inauguration. I had Joseph Kennedy on board and Sandra Day O'Connor on board, and I served as a former Vice President of the United States.

It was a Minneapolis-Tokyo flight, and during the briefing, it was noted that we would be flying a VIP. The senior Flight Attendants bid for Business Class and upper deck, but I ended up being the relief lead during the breaks. My service position during the breaks would be upper deck which was where the former Vice President Walter Mondale and his secret service people were seated. They occupied the entire upper deck cabin. It was quiet in the upper deck cabin, and the former Vice President slept while the security team kept a watchful eye.

I was working a domestic flight with Clare departing Memphis when I recognized the distinctive walk of Dixie Carter as she sashayed down the aisle. I could only see her from behind, but doing the aisle check, sure enough there she was. During the service, she was seated in the Clares section, and this was around the time she was doing the Coffeemate commercials. When Clare took her drink order, she asked for coffee. Clare, being Clare, shot back, "Would you like Coffeemate with that?" Dixie Carter, always the class act, gave her a smile.

I was flying lead on an Airbus trip from Detroit to Atlanta. I noticed someone seated in the main cabin who looked familiar to me, but I could not place the face or the place. I checked the Spill, which listed all passenger names, and the name listed in his seat was Benjamin Knox. I felt I recognized the person, and my curiosity peaked, so I decided to talk to him. I took a trash bag to disguise my intentions and picked up cups as I headed down the aisle. I reached his seat, looked at him, and smiled. He smiled back. "Can I get you anything, Mr. Knox?" He looked up as if surprised I knew his name. "Oh, no, thank you, baby," he replied. When I heard that voice, I knew exactly who this was. He was Lady Chablis from Midnight in The Garden of Good and Evil. I kneeled by his seat to have a short chat, and he appeared so grateful that I had taken the time to acknowledge his performance and the entertainer that he was. He invited me to his show in Savannah if I could ever make it. He was a kind and talented man who sadly passed away in 2016.

One of the last, but certainly not the least, of the celebrities I had on board was on a Detroit to Minneapolis. We had the white Target Dog with the red bullseye around the eye. He sat quietly in Seat 1C at the bulkhead as his trainer seated beside him held on to him during takeoff and landing.

In every flight Attendant career, there have been times you were asked questions that had no logic or reason or could not possibly have a satisfactory answer. Always the Diplomat, you had to produce some sort of answer, truthful or otherwise. At times it would appear passengers could suddenly go stupid at the boarding door. There were moments when I felt like some passengers, along with the price of their tickets, felt they had paid for the Flight Attendants to think for them. Passenger: "Where is row sixteen?" FA: "Oh, keep going. You are headed in the right direction," as you point to the seat numbers on the overhead bins. What you are thinking, however, is, "It's right behind row fifteen, just before row seventeen."

Passenger: sitting across from the jump seat. "Looks like your company thinks more of you than they do of me with you in such a big, protected seat." FA: "I am sure you must think that but do keep in mind we are here for your safety. If we don't get out of the aircraft in an emergency, you won't." What you are thinking, however, is, "You might want to rethink that question."

Passenger: Flying over the North Atlantic at night at thirty-five thousand feet. "Where are we?" FA: "Oh, we are over the North Atlantic, flying at a high altitude." What you are thinking is, "It's the middle of the night. We are high over the Atlantic Ocean, and how is this question relevant?"

I can honestly say working a flight with a passenger load of up to four hundred can be highly stressful. In my years of flying, for me, the best stress reliever was humor. I believe it is important to be able to laugh and to be able to laugh at oneself. Boarding the aircraft has always been and continues to be the most stressful part of any flight. Tempers flare, and things happen with people frantic to stow entirely too much carry-on in small places. I was at the boarding door on a widebody aircraft headed for Amsterdam. A college age boy is stooped down in the aisle, oblivious that his pants and underwear have slipped down, and he was giving those boarding the aircraft a full moon. The galley Fight Attendant sees the situation and whispers in my ear, "Just say no to crack." Always, humor would save the day. On another flight I was handed a paper towel full of nail clippings from a Business Class passenger. I tried not to show it, but this was so lacking in sensibility that it was cringe-worthy. As I stepped into the galley, I was asked by the galley Flight Attendant what was wrong. I showed her what I was disposing of, and she said while shaking her head, "Somebody needs to tell that passenger that we are here to save her ass, not kiss it."

I was in the lead position working a DC9 trip from Memphis to Charlotte, and a woman took her assigned seat in row two in First Class. This was scheduled to be a quick beverage flight, and I expected a routine, easy flight. Wrong: I began to take beverage orders, and when I got to her seat, she asked what I would be serving for lunch. I explained to her that any flight under three hours flight time was beverage only. With this, she exploded! The more I apologized, the angrier she got. "I have not had anything to eat all morning because I thought this would be a meal flight. Do I need to book my flight with someone else in the future? What is this a hillbilly hayride?" "No, Mame, but for that, you "would" need to book with someone else, but may I get you a beverage?" I said as I offered her the snack basket. This woman was one of those passengers I call a lose-lose. Nothing you say or do will make the situation better. The best you can do is the best you can do.

I had someone tell me once, "I can tell you are a Flight Attendant." This gave me a laugh, and I pushed back. "Really, how so?" She told me it was the way I carried myself. I had to smile at this. Some Flight Attendants might carry themselves like an uncorseted sack of potatoes, while others may be refined and dignified. I never saw myself as either. There was one issue that struck me as odd. My family always made jokes about it, but I could be in a store, on the street, or even in a group, and someone would approach me with questions as if I worked there. Did they think I had all the answers?

Flight Attendants often find themselves in odd situations, happenings that could come from out of the blue. One layover in Raleigh, I decided to go to the Piggly Wiggly supermarket which was right around the corner from my layover hotel. While picking out the few items I needed to take back to my room, I noticed a large woman in a jean skirt and bulky blouse who seemed to be carefully shopping as she slowly moved down the meat counter. I got in the check-out line and waited. I noticed the same lady was heading for the door. Suddenly, I heard a thud that sounded like meat hitting the floor. The checkers and customers looked in her direction. It looked like a twelve-pound ham had dropped from under her skirt. She had a look of shock as she looked over her shoulder. She then realized the whole store had seen what had happened. She loudly shouted, "Who threw that ham at me? I'm never coming in this store again." She then hurried out the door. Even the checkers were laughing as the ham remained on the floor until one of the sackers scooped it up. I looked at the checker and asked. "You're not going to put that back on the shelf, are you?"

It seemed like every base had one colleague or crew member who was intentionally and habitually annoying. For me it was a Seattle-based Flight Attendant I called "The Flying Flea." He was an irritation wherever and whenever he went. When we saw this man coming, we all knew to run for our lives. He was trouble. He was vertically challenged but certainly not verbally challenged. He would create drama and dissension between an otherwise smoothly working crew with each flight he worked. On a nine-hour international flight, he could create so much dissention with he said, she said whispering campaign the crews would not be speaking to one another on landing. Leads would try to address the situation in briefings, not mentioning names, by speaking about the need to work together as a team. "If anyone has a problem with a fellow crew member, please address that problem directly to the one or ones involved." This went right over his head, never acknowledging he was the problem, never the solution. Something must have happened to the "Flying Flea." Fortunately, I never saw him again in my last two months of flying out of the Seattle base. It was whispered he had been fired, but no one seemed to know for sure. In many cases Karma will step in to solve a problem that seemed impossible to resolve.

25

Always Tomorrow

The Airline Industry is all about change, innovation, modern technology, new procedures, and newer and better practices. For the last few decades, from the so-called "Golden Age," more and more of the world has been flying. Safety procedures have been enhanced, and there are more flights that take off and land safely than ever before. However, from the seventies onward, from hijackings to terrorist attacks, it is the airline industry that has been weaponized as an element of hate. With each terrorist attack or targeted aircraft, we step up and refine our security measures. We try to create a safe and secure flight for passengers and crew, but very often, after each incident, Airlines, crews, and employees pay the price. Passenger loads fall off, route systems are cut back, and planes are grounded. There is no other industry so directly impacted by these tragedies than Aviation. After Lockerbie, 911, The Shoe Bomber, and more, passengers did not fly. This always resulted in reductions in force or layoffs. It is when a recovery starts to kick in that something like Covid knocks the world back once again. Now, it is systematic cyber-attacks, and again, Aviation pays the price. Yes, it is a cyclical business, and adjustments will always be necessary, but each of these setbacks involves the lives of thousands of airline workers and crews.

Through it all, Flight Attendants have been there. Those senior, grey-haired men and women who continue to show up for every flight have seen it all and then some. There is no other job in this country that is more scrutinized and regulated than the position of a Flight Attendant. They have gone through vigorous initial training and are required to complete mandatory competency training once every year. They are randomly drug and alcohol tested, all in the name of safety. With this training and this scrutiny comes responsibility and, hard work, and also a certain amount of courage.

In this age of flying, Flight Attendants are expected to always do more with less and to do it faster and better than ever before. They face expanded expectations and seem to always rise to the occasion.

When I began my career with Northwest Airlines, Flight Attendants had a list of required items to have with them at all times. Flashlights and a working wrist watch as well as a wine opener to name a few. We were required to handle unruly passengers with diplomacy and tact. Now passenger incidents are so prevalent it seems like the most required items should be a whip and a chair. Flight Attendants are more and more required to be referees. They are called upon to settle disputes about seat assignments. The passengers today are no longer as dignified, well-dressed, and polite as they once were. Those days are long gone. Flight Attendants today are sometimes called upon when a passenger complains about the hygiene and smell of the passenger seated next to them. What can be done when there are no available seats to move to? It can sometimes look like it is the Flight attendant problem because the situation could not be resolved. Problems aside, there seem to be more and more passengers traveling these days that could benefit from a flea dip. Overweight seating as well. As the seats have gotten smaller and the passengers have gotten larger, there seem to be more complaints about the girth of one passenger encroaching on another when it is a full aircraft, again no solution other than seat belt extenders, which only protects the problem but doesn't help with a solution.

When I fly today, I am in awe of the flight crews, their patience during the boarding process, and their teamwork during the service. I know what they have been through to get where they are. I think about those senior crews I worked with when I first started flying and how I envied their seniority. That seniority would be mine had I continued to fly, and those new hires would be envious of me. So, the cycle goes. For my classmates and colleagues who started when I did and are still flying, you have my admiration and respect. Your seniority has been well earned.

Both Clare and Christine have continued to fly and are a treasured member of the Delta Family.

Michael left Northwest after several years and continues to fly. He remains a shining star at a company he loves.

Epilogue

We each have a dream. That dream is special because it belongs to only us. It is ours alone. All that matters is how we make that dream come true. My dream was to be a Flight Attendant.

If I could hold a mirror to the face of my younger self and ask him if he would do anything differently, I know his answer would be no. He would change nothing! His dream came true and more.

Palm Springs is known as God's waiting room, and this may be true, but we are all waiting for something. I am waiting for the next adventure, that next trip to somewhere, anywhere, for the next chapter of my life.

In the mornings, I sit by my pool with the mountain view and wait for the Sun to rise in the east. My house sets in the direct take-off pattern of the flights departing Palm Spring Airport. I can hear the morning bank of departures overhead as I watch the planes descend into the western sky. I can close my eyes and visualize those Flight Attendants strapped into their jump seats. I smile to think that used to be me. For those who are still flying, I say take a bow and take another for a job well done. For all those future flights, I wish you well, and most importantly, I wish you safe landings.

I was once asked how I felt about flying for Northwest Airlines? My answer was I feel lucky and grateful. Lucky that Northwest helped make my dreams come true, and grateful to be a part of such a special company.

Northwest Airlines gave me a gift, and they gave me the gift of the world. For this, I will always be grateful.

David Edmondson

Palm Springs California

In Memorium

Maria Brulewiez

John Davenport

John Dewitt

Tommie Parker

Karen Voelcker Rath

Karl Reinhold

The sky has been a lonelier place without you…

Visit David @..<u>dewriteoutloud.com</u>